teach® yourself

basic Mac skills

rod lawton

Launched in 1938, the **teach yourself** series grew rapidly in response to the world's wartime needs. Loved and trusted by over 50 million readers, the series has continued to respond to society's changing interests and passions and now, 70 years on, includes over 500 titles, from Arabic and Beekeeping to Yoga and Zulu. What would you like to learn?

Be where you want to be with **teach yourself**

For UK order enquiries: please contact Bookpoint Ltd, 130 Milton Park, Abingdon, Oxon OX14 4SB. Telephone: +44 (0)1235 827720. Fax: +44 (0)1235 400454. Lines are open 09.00– 17.00, Monday to Saturday, with a 24-hour message answering service. Details about our titles and how to order are available at www.teachyourself.co.uk.

For USA order enquiries: please contact McGraw-Hill Customer Services, PO Box 545, Blacklick, OH 43004-0545, USA. Telephone: 1-800-722-4726. Fax: 1-614-755-5645.

For Canada order enquiries: please contact McGraw-Hill Ryerson Ltd, 300 Water St, Whitby, Ontario L1N 9B6, Canada. Telephone: 905 430 5000. Fax: 905 430 5020.

Long renowned as the authoritative source for self-guided learning – with more than 50 million copies sold worldwide – the **teach yourself** series includes over 500 titles in the fields of languages, crafts, hobbies, business, computing and education.

British Library Cataloguing in Publication Data: a catalogue record for this title is available from The British Library.

Library of Congress Catalog Card Number: on file.

First published in UK 2008 by Hodder Education, part of Hachette Livre UK, 338 Euston Road, London NW1 3BH.

First published in US 2008 by The McGraw-Hill Companies, Inc.

The **teach yourself** name is a registered trademark of Hodder Headline.

Computer hardware and software brand names mentioned in this book are protected by their respective trademarks and are acknowledged.

Typeset by MacDesign, Southampton

Printed in Great Britain for Hodder Education, a division of Hodder Headline, an Hachette Livre UK Company, 338 Euston Road, London NW1 3BH, by Cox & Wyman Ltd, Reading, Berkshire.

The publisher has used its best endeavours to ensure that the URLs for external websites referred to in this book are correct and active at the time of going to press. However, the publisher and the author have no responsibility for the websites and can make no guarantee that a site will remain live or that the content will remain relevant, decent or appropriate.

Hachette Livre UK's policy is to use papers that are natural, renewable and recyclable products and made from wood grown in sustainable forests. The logging and manufacturing processes are expected to conform to the environmental regulations of the country of origin.

Impression number   10 9 8 7 6 5 4 3 2 1

Year   2012 2011 2010 2009 2008

contents

preface

Why you should read this

If you're anything like us, a book's Preface is the last thing you're going to read. You just want to get on with it. But we would urge you to read this – it really won't take long.

About you

You may have just bought your first Mac, or be thinking of buying a Mac. Or you may simply be curious about how Macs work and what they can do. Whichever it is, this book is for you. It will help if you have some basic computer experience, but it's not essential. This book isn't designed for experts and, in any case, there is a glossary of common computing terms at the back.

How this book works

First, this book is not a manual. An exhaustive (and exhausting) reference to every single Mac application, toolbar, function and setting would produce a book big enough to stop your car rolling down a hill and dull enough to cure an army of insomniacs.

That's not what the Mac is about. As Apple continues to demonstrate with every new launch, the Mac is all about helping you with your life. The suite of applications that comes installed on Macs is called 'iLife', which is a bit of a clue in itself.

The iLife applications are designed, first and foremost, to make everyday computing jobs simple. And clear. And useful. And that's what we've tried to do with this book, too.

Explaining every single menu command doesn't help. You want to know what you can do, whether it's easy and how to get started. The main thing is understanding, and everything hangs on that. So what we've done is concentrate on the broad explanations – the understanding part – and thrown in some simple step-by-steps to get you started with those everyday tasks.

What's been left out

So we've left out those long, technical dissections. We've also left out Apple's pro applications and the role of the Mac in the creative professions. We'll save that for another book. This one's for home/office users who either have a Mac or are thinking of getting one and want to know more about it.

It would have been nice to have done a whole chapter on iChat and its remarkable 'theatre' mode. Can you believe that you can show someone else, in another country, what you're doing on your computer and even take control of theirs, in a real-time video conversation?

And we didn't have room for GarageBand, a music program so simple and yet so sophisticated that it's practically a revolution. It's breathtaking for being (a) so good and (b) free, as standard, with any new Mac.

Tiger or Leopard?

This book's been based on the lastest version of the Mac operating system, OS X 10.5 'Leopard'. But the change from Tiger (OS X 10.4) to Leopard is not of the same magnitude as the change from Windows XP to Vista.

If you've got a Mac running Tiger, most of the content of this book will still apply because the latest iLife and iWork suites are available separately, and work in just the same way on either operating system.

And you know what? Tiger is still rather good. You don't have to upgrade if you don't want to because there's a lot of life left in the big cat yet.

01

choosing a Mac

In this chapter you will learn:

- about the hardware specifications
- how much memory and hard disk space you need
- who the different Mac models are designed for
- which Mac is best for you
- about Mac versus PCs: the facts

1.1 Processors

Choosing a computer is complicated if you have little interest in technicalities, and it's not much better even if you do know the difference between a processor and a peripheral, because the benchmarks are moving all the time. Besides, what's touted as a 'revolution' often turns out to be just a slight improvement on what went before. Don't forget that the primary purpose of any computer manufacturer is to sell more computers!

But you do need something to go on when weighing up one model versus another and deciding what to spend. And computers are generally judged on three components: the processor, the memory (RAM) and the hard disk size. These are the components that always head up the specs sheets in the store.

We'll start with the processor, which can be considered to be the computer's 'brain'. Processors are evolving all the time, and what's hot this year (dual core) will be next year's budget buy, so don't try to memorize the figures, just remember the principles.

Three things affect the processor performance: (a) the processor *family* (each generation is a leap forward from the last), (b) the *operating system* and *hardware* of the computer it's running on and (c) its *clock speed*, which is the rate at which it performs calculations.

For example, if we go to the Apple website and check the specs of the cheapest Mac Mini we find that at the time of writing it has a Core 2 Duo processor (that's the chip family) running at 1.83GHz (*gigahertz* – that's the clock speed). By contrast, the top-of-the-range iMac has a Core 2 Duo Extreme processor (same family, but improved) running at 2.8GHz (almost twice the speed). We can expect the expensive iMac to work considerably faster than the cheap Mac Mini, then.

Mac Pros use a different processor family. Dual-core processors (two chips in one, essentially) aren't powerful enough for the high-end creative applications these computers are designed for, and they use a different quad-core chip family. In the top model these run at a speed of 3.0GHz – not much faster than the top iMac – but the quad-core design is intrinsically more powerful than the dual-core processor in the iMac.

Confused? Let's keep it simple, then. A better chip family usually gives you the biggest performance improvement, but if two computers use the same processor family, then you can judge which is the faster from the clock speed.

You can visit the Apple Store via www.apple.com/uk to see the range of Mac configurations available. This makes it clearer how the range is broken down.

1.2 RAM

Processor speed, though, is not the sole factor in deciding performance. It doesn't matter how fast the computer's brain is if it has a tiny memory.

This is the RAM, or *Random Access Memory*. It's like the computer's thinking space. The more RAM it has the more things it can do at once.

All computers, Macs included, are sold with enough RAM to get you started, but they always work better with more. It is possible to buy and fit more RAM chips yourself, but it may be simpler to specify more memory when you order the machine – this prevents any quibbles over whether you've opened the machine up inside the warranty period.

Mac Minis come with 1Gb RAM, which is actually adequate for most purposes, but there's space inside to increase this to 2Gb. That's a minimum for many professional applications, but the Mac Mini isn't aimed at this market.

iMacs also ship with 1Gb RAM. That's a little on the low side, not because they demand more RAM, but because their users are likely to be a little more ambitious in what they do and the programs they want to run. The amount of RAM, though, can be increased up to 4Gb.

Mac Pros also come with 1Gb of RAM in their basic configuration. That's not enough for professional users, who will almost certainly order extra or fit it themselves. These machines can accommodate up to 16Gb of RAM.

So how much do you need? Well, for email, surfing, the iLife applications that come with the computer and general office jobs like word processing and so on, 1Gb is fine. If you're interested in digital photography or digital video, you're probably going to be better off with 2Gb of RAM. Professional applications in these areas are likely to work a little faster with 4Gb of RAM, especially if you are running more than one program at the same time. Beyond that you're into specialist territory that's outside the scope of this book.

Now the point about RAM is that if you don't have enough, you don't usually find that things refuse to work. That's because the Mac will get the extra memory it needs by temporarily using space on the hard disk – this is *virtual memory*. It's a neat idea that's also used by Windows on PCs. The problem is that by comparison with real (RAM) memory, it's terribly slow. Imagine you have a very poor memory yourself (maybe you don't need to imagine!) and you have to keep stopping what you're doing to write it down so that you can clear your mind for something else. That's what the computer's doing with virtual memory. It will work much faster if it doesn't have to keep stopping to write data to the disk and then read it back into the memory again later on.

Indeed, the amount of RAM can be just as big a factor in the computer's performance as the processor it uses. If you don't have enough RAM, your super-fast processor is going to spend much of its time kicking its heels and waiting for data.

1.3 Hard disk size

The third big selling point of computers is the hard disk size. Where the RAM is for 'thinking space', the hard disk is for permanent storage.

Hard disk size is measured in Gb (gigabytes) and the basic Mac Mini comes with an 80Gb hard disk, while the top iMac has a 320Mb hard disk, though it can be ordered with a 1Tb (*terabyte* = 1000 gigabytes) drive too.

That's all very well, but how big a hard disk do you need? That will depend on what you use your computer for, but by the time you've installed a couple of extra programs, built up a photo collection and maybe stored some movie clips, copied your CD collection into iTunes and accumulated a few months' worth of letters, homework assignments and other documents, there's not going to be a lot of free space left on an 80Gb drive.

The 250Gb drive in basic iMacs is a good starting point, and it'll take some time to fill up a disk of this size. Unfortunately, that's not an option on Mac Minis and the Mac laptops because they use physically smaller drives (they have to be smaller to fit the space available) with smaller maximum capacities. With these models, though, you can always increase the available storage space with an external disk drive.

The Mac Pro is a special case. It's a professional machine which means it must be versatile and expandable. It can accommodate more than one hard disk – in fact there are bays for up to four hard disks, and these can be used for extra storage space, or for data backups.

1.4   Getting started: the Mac Mini

Now that we've explained the three main specifications for computers, it's going to be easier to examine the individual Macs in the range and their suitability for particular jobs. And we'll start with the Mac Mini, the cheapest Mac of all.

This is unlike any other computer you'll see. It's smaller than you might imagine if you've only ever seen it in pictures, and in fact it's only about 50% larger than a CD case, though quite a lot thicker.

The Mac Mini is perfect for PC owners who are undecided about making the switch to the Mac. It's sold without a keyboard, mouse or monitor, but the idea is that you supply your own.

You simply unplug the cables from your current PC and plug them into the Mac instead. There may be a couple of setup adjustments you need to make along the way, and you may need an adaptor for the monitor, but that's the extent of any technical difficulties. (You will also need a USB keyboard and mouse.)

This, together with the modest hardware specifications, makes the Mac Mini cheap to buy. It's supremely practical, too, because you'll no longer be banging your knees on a huge tower system under your desk – the Mac mini is small enough to squeeze on to even the most cramped and cluttered computer desk.

The modest specification means that it's not the quickest Mac on the market, but it's no slouch. The fact is that most of the things we use a computer for don't really require much in the way of computing power. If you're mostly interested in email, surfing, word processing and experimenting with the bundled iLife programs, it really is all you need. An iMac, for example, will certainly be a bit quicker, but not in any great life-changing sort of way.

If you want to try a Mac but you're not sure about committing a lot of cash, the Mac Mini is the one to buy. It might look like a toy, but it's nothing of the sort – it's a real computer of considerable ability.

The Mac Mini is a 'starter' Mac for those who already have a keyboard, mouse and monitor. It's seen here with Apple's standard-issue remote control (photos: courtesy of Apple).

1.5 Family workhorse: the iMac

Good as it is, the Mac Mini is still a kind of stopgap for those who are still undecided about committing fully to the Mac. The fact is that the iMac is a better all-round computer for a number of reasons.

The first is that it comes with faster processors and the option of fitting more RAM. It also has a decent-sized hard disk – and this is one of the Mac Mini's failings. Perhaps the main point, though, is that it's built into the back of the monitor, so you get an extremely elegant computer which doesn't actually have a base unit at all.

Apple's monitors are very good. By the time you've bought one separately, and of comparable quality, to go with a Mac Mini, you're getting close to the cost of a basic iMac. Besides, the iMac comes with a mouse and keyboard as standard – the Mac Mini comes with neither.

The iMac is perfect for use in the home because it's powerful, stylish and practical – there is no base unit because the computing hardware is built into the monitor (photo: courtesy of Apple).

The latest version of the iMac has a brushed aluminium finish and a slimline aluminium keyboard. It's a very stylish machine, and if you've got to have a computer in your living room, then you (or your partner) are going to want one that looks good.

Many computer users will be unimpressed and will point instead to how much cheaper a comparable PC system is. It's perfectly true. You have to decide how much you value style over cost. But don't imagine that 'style' is all the iMac has to offer. The minimalist design isn't just to look good. It takes up less space, and uses far fewer cables. You get a much clearer, cleaner environment to work in.

This is why the iMac is the best Mac for home users. And don't worry that it doesn't have quite the power of the Mac Pro. Whenever there's another, more expensive model further up in the range, it generates a kind of 'performance anxiety' that puts you off the cheaper one. Forget it. For most jobs, the Mac Pro will provide no discernible performance advantage. Indeed, the top-end iMacs are worthy alternatives to low-end Mac Pros. There's no sharp dividing line – it's more like a broad area of crossover.

1.6 Creative professionals: Mac Pro

The Mac Pro is for those who must have both performance and expandability; users for whom even the fastest computer is still too slow, and who may require specialized computing hardware for their particular field.

In addition to its fast quad-core processors, the Mac Pro can be fitted with a maximum of 16Gb RAM and four hard disk drives. It's a big machine, but that's because it must have space inside for additional components, as required, and it must be easy to open up so that hardware can be fitted.

It's the sort of machine that might be chosen by professional photographers, videographers and designers, particularly those working in 3D design and animation. But unless you know for sure that you're going to need every ounce of power that modern computing technology (and a lot of cash!) can provide, it's probably overkill.

The Mac Pro is the most powerful Mac of all, and comes as a large aluminium tower. Monitors, like the one seen here, have to be bought separately (photo: courtesy of Apple).

1.7 The portable MacBook

The Macs we've looked at so far are all static desktop machines. Apple also makes two ranges of laptops: the MacBook and the MacBook Pro. As the names suggest, they're aimed at general users and professionals respectively.

The MacBook is currently available in either white or black. Our advice? Get the white. It's a no-brainer. The while version has the classically elegant look that Apple's become famous for, while the black one looks like a rather hideous and overpriced copy of Windows laptops half the price. A superficial judgement, certainly, but many choose Macs for their looks, so it's got to be taken seriously.

MacBooks come with 13" widescreen displays. That's smaller than the screen on any PC laptop, but you shouldn't be put off by this. Macs use high-resolution displays and, unless you have trouble reading small text, the screen on the MacBook is easily big enough. Besides, it allows a much slimmer design. Not only is the MacBook thin, it's short from front-to-back, too. When the display hinges back, you don't immediately shut out everyone else in the room, and you don't get that slightly unstable top-heaviness that can affect other laptops.

There are three basic configurations, though these can be modified manually if you order from the Apple Store online – you can order a bigger hard disk, for example, or more RAM.

The basic model has a Core 2 Duo processor, 1Gb RAM and an 80Gb hard disk drive. This is adequate for most purposes, but if you can afford the extra, you'll be better off long-term with a 160Gb hard disk (the biggest you can get) and 2Gb RAM.

The MacBook makes an excellent portable computer, and while the 13" display might sound small, it's actually perfectly fine. Make sure you get the white finish rather than black – it's much nicer-looking (photo: courtesy of Apple).

1.8 Professional portability: the MacBook Pro

Professional users may need a bigger screen, more RAM (the MacBook only goes up to 2Gb) and a bigger hard disk. That's where the MacBook Pro comes in, and there are two models, distinguished by their screen size – the 15" and the 17". Apart from the larger screen, the 17" model can accommodate a larger hard disk (250Gb maximum versus 200GB in the 15"). Both models come with 2Gb RAM but can be fitted with up to 4Gb.

The MacBook Pro is Apple's professional laptop. It comes in an aluminium finish and with a 15" or 17" display (photo: courtesy of Apple).

If you just need a general-purpose personal computer, the standard MacBook will do the job perfectly. But if you're a designer, an artist, an animator or are involved in any kind of creative business, a MacBook Pro will be the better choice because the demands of the job and the software you use will be higher.

1.9 Graphics cards, and DVD-writers

We haven't mentioned graphics cards yet. These are another big selling point for computers, but more so for PCs than Macs. One of the main reasons for getting a powerful graphics card is so that games display better – animation will be smoother, detail will be finer and backgrounds more realistic.

It's also important to point out that the reason games need high-powered graphics cards is that they have to manipulate virtual 3D objects in real-time. This is not the same as displaying static photos or playing back movies and DVDs, which consist of frames which have already been created, or *rendered*. There's no complex maths involved here.

What we're getting round to saying is that all Macs will display photos and videos at high resolution and perfectly smoothly, regardless of the graphics cards they're fitted with. It's only 3D games where it may make a difference, and few people buy Macs to play games on. That's why we've not gone into great depth about graphics cards in this book.

It is possible to get many Mac games, but it's not a games machine in the way that PCs are. It's probably fair to say that anyone really keen on games will get a games console or a PC to play them on. It's not really what the Mac's about. (Apologies to any hardcore 3D Mac gamers out there who we've just offended, but you must see what we mean.)

High-powered graphics cards will also be important to 3D designers and perhaps videographers, but this is professional territory outside the scope of this book.

When comparing Macs, check to see whether you're getting a *combo drive* or a *superdrive*. Combo drives can read CDs and DVDs, but they can only write CDs. If you want to write DVDs too, you need a Mac with a superdrive. You may find that the cheapest model in the range comes with a combo drive and you have to get the next one up to get a superdrive.

Having said that, although a DVD writer sounds a useful thing to have in principle, you might go weeks, months or years without actually using it. They're handy for those who want to send home movies to friends and relatives, but don't have many other practical uses.

1.10 Mac vs PC: time to stop arguing!

When you're shopping for a Mac it's likely you will encounter many arguments in the Mac versus PC debate, particularly if you're asking around to find out which one you ought to buy. It's rare to find people who have used both for long enough to form an opinion, and as a result you tend to get unbalanced and sometimes grossly distorted viewpoints.

The principal arguments against Macs from PC fans are broadly as follows:

•   They cost a lot more

•   You don't get the same power as a PC at the same price

- They're only for designers and 'creatives'
- You can't get the software
- They're all style and no substance
- They're not as versatile as PCs

There is some truth in some of these arguments, but they also overlook the Mac's strengths.

Firstly, it's difficult to compare the relative performance of Macs and PCs at the same price because they use different operating systems and different applications. Whatever test you use, someone will argue that it's been weighted towards one machine or the other. Broadly, though, PCs may give you faster processing at a specific price point. It's certainly true that you can buy good, fast, up-to-date PCs for less than the price of an iMac or a MacBook, say.

The next notion, though, that Macs are only for designers, is long out of date. The professional design community has long preferred Macs, that's true, but all along Apple's specialities have been innovation, elegance and ease of use. And nowhere is this more obvious than its latest suite of iLife and iWork applications. These are not only cheap (free, in the case of iLife), they are also exceptionally good. We all imagine that free or bundled software must be cheap, old or ineffective, but the Apple applications are none of these. What's more, they are all clearly part of the same family and work together and not just as separate applications.

This changes the cost equation, too. The software provided free with Macs is very much better than people imagine 'free' software to be.

This affects the other suggestion, that you 'can't get the software'. Well, given that Macs already come with iPhoto, iCal, iTunes, iDVD, iMovie, Garage Band, Mail and Safari, the question is how much more you actually need. All high-end design software is, as you'd expect given its reputation, available on the Mac, and if you want to use the Mac in business you can get iWork (just £55 in the UK) or the Mac version of Microsoft Office. Oh yes, there is a Mac version.

It is true that there aren't as many software packages for the Mac as there are the PC, and that you might have to buy via mail order because most computer retailers don't stock them. In practice, though, the major applications in specific fields are generally available for both computers.

Besides, with the release of Leopard, if the worst comes to the worst you can always buy a copy of Windows and start up your Mac as a PC for those applications which don't come in Mac versions at all.

Style-wise, it's true that Apple puts a great deal of effort into the design of both its computers and its software, and it seems reasonable to argue that money spent here could have been spent on reducing the price or increasing the features. It's an argument you could have about any consumer item. Would you rather have cheap clothes or nice ones? Exactly. You don't have to base your buying decisions on ruthless practicality. You are allowed to choose things you actually like.

Finally, there's the question of versatility. Yes – hands up – PCs are more versatile. They can do a wider range of things, use a wider range of software and can be expanded with a wider range of specialist hardware.

Can you get the software? Macs come with a large number of programs pre-installed, and are very well supported with pro-level 'creative' applications like the 'Aperture' photo management program (courtesy of Apple).

But this is not something that everyone wants to do or needs to. You might be advised to buy a PC just in case you need to do these things in the future, but will you? Really? It's like buying a van instead of a car just in case you need to carry something big one day.

Summary

+ Processors come in different 'families'.

+ Processor speed (gigahertz) is important, but not as important as the family.

+ Extra RAM will improve performance (like any computer, in fact).

+ The smaller hard disk options on MacBooks and Mac Minis will fill up quickly.

+ The cheap Mac Mini is the perfect 'toe-in-the-water' Mac.

+ The iMac is the perfect family workhorse.

+ The Mac Pro is only needed by professional designers.

+ The MacBook is perfect as an everyday laptop, while the MacBook Pro is better for professional designers.

+ If you want to be able to write DVDs, check the Mac has a superdrive.

+ Macs may appear to cost more than PCs, but you're getting rather more than you might think.

02 how Macs work

In this chapter you will learn:

- how Macs start up
- about the items on the Desktop
- basic mouse skills
- about menus, windows and dialogs
- how to use the Dock
- how to open files and run programs
- how to use the Finder
- what to do if your Mac crashes
- about shutdown and sleep mode

2.1 Starting up

Macs may seem very different from PCs, especially if you go by what you've heard, but in fact one computer is, at heart, very much like another. And this is certainly true of Macs and PCs, which start up in a very similar fashion.

1 When you press the power button, the Mac goes through a series of basic hardware checks to make sure everything's working properly. This is when you hear the characteristic Mac 'chime'.

2 The Mac now loads the operating system from the hard disk. This is standard practice for all computers – the operating system is what controls the user interface and how programs and accessories work alongside the computer hardware. On the Mac, the operating system is OS X, on the PC it's Windows.

3 Loading the operating system takes quite a few seconds, during which you'll see the Mac loading screen. When the OS has finished loading, the Mac will display the Desktop.

The Mac's desktop has an icon for its hard disk (top right) and a 'dock' running along the bottom which you can use to start programs or switch between them.

2.2 The Desktop

The Desktop on the Mac is just like a real Desktop. You use it to arrange the items you're working on at the moment, and you can either leave them out (in which case their icons will still be on the Desktop the next time you start the Mac up), or file them neatly away in folders – just like using a filing cabinet or desk drawers in an office.

The Mac Desktop has two items that are always visible. One is the *Macintosh HD* icon which represents the hard disk inside the Mac. You can double-click this to display its contents. The other is the Dock at the bottom of the screen. This has icons (buttons) for various programs installed on your Mac.

2.3 Basic mouse skills

Like PCs, Macs are controlled using a mouse. When you move the mouse, a pointer moves around on the screen. There are a series of mouse actions which are fundamental to controlling computers, and while these might seem complicated at first, they'll soon become second nature.

*   **Clicking:** you do this to select an object on the screen, press a button or open a menu (by clicking on its title). Just move the mouse pointer over the object, button or menu, and press the mouse button once. Strictly speaking, we should call this 'left-clicking', because some mice have two buttons, left and right. The Apple Mighty Mouse is a little different from PC mice because it only has one button (this does have two 'sides' but usually it's not set up to use the right side).

*   **Double-clicking:** to do this, click on an object twice in quick succession. This may take a little practice initially. If you get the gap between the clicks right, this double-click action launches an icon. If it's a program icon, it starts the program; if it's a file icon, it opens the file using the relevant program.

*   **Dragging:** this is used to move objects around the screen. You move the mouse pointer over the object and press the button, but don't release it. Instead, you keep the button pressed as you move the mouse. The object is selected and follows the mouse pointer as you move it around the screen.

You might do this to move a document from one folder to another, for example, or drag the title bar of a window to move it to a different position on the screen.

*   **Scrolling**: this is where you use the wheel that many mice have on the top to scroll up and down through documents or web pages. The Apple Mighty Mouse has a little ball rather than a wheel, but it works in the same way. Windows also have scroll bars which you can use to move around the document too.

*   **Right-clicking**: this is used to display *shortcut* or *context* menus relevant to the item you've clicked on. The alternative, for those using single-button mice or who can't get the hang of right-clicking, is to hold down the Mac's **[Ctrl]** key as you left-click. This has the same effect.

If you're new to computers you'll have to spend a little while learning basic Mac skills like 'clicking', 'double-clicking' and 'dragging'.

Picture 1

2.4   Menus, dialogs and windows

Menus are at the heart of most applications on the Mac, just as they are on the PC. A menu is a list of options which opens up when you click on the menu title. On the Mac, the menus run along the top of the screen in a *menu bar*, although some *windows*, *dialogs* and *palettes* have small pop-up menus too.

To open a menu, you click on its title with the mouse. Then you move the mouse down the list to find the command you need. (Some of these commands open out into 'submenus'.) As soon as you select a menu option, the menu closes.

Menus appear at the top of the screen. When you click the menu title, a vertical list of options appears below – you click on the one you want.

Some commands carry out an action straight away. Others call up dialogs with further choices. For example, if you select some text in Microsoft Word and choose a different font from the **Font** menu, it's applied to the text straight away. But if you use the **File > Save As** command, the program needs more information before it can proceed, so it displays the **Save** dialog, where you choose a new name for the file and the location where you want it stored. To put it simply, when the Mac needs more information before it can proceed, it displays a dialog.

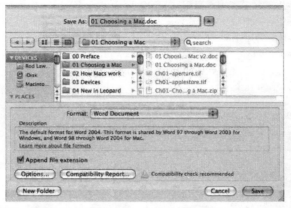

When the Mac needs more information from you before it can proceed, it displays a dialog.

The files you work on are displayed in windows. You can usually work on more than one file at once, and each will have its own window. These can be moved around the screen – you just drag the window's title bar which runs horizontally along the top. You can change the size of a window by dragging its bottom right-hand corner, and close a window by clicking the red button in the top left-hand corner. The yellow button next to it *minimizes* the window to the Dock without actually closing it, while the green button to the right of that optimizes the window size to fit the document you're working on.

The documents and other items you work on are show in 'windows', which can be resized and moved around the screen.

A window won't necessarily be able to show the whole of a document, in which case you'll see a *scrollbar* running vertically down the right-hand side of the window with a blue bar which you can drag up and down to scroll up and down the document. The small grey button on top of a Mighty Mouse can be used for vertical scrolling too. Occasionally, the document may be too wide for the window, for example when you zoom in on a digital photo. Here, you'll see a horizontal scrollbar running across the bottom of the window. This works in the same way as the vertical scrollbar.

Many Mac applications use *toolbars*. These usually run horizontally across the top of the screen directly under the menu bar. They contain a mixture of buttons and drop-down menus designed to make common tasks easier to carry out, partly by making them more accessible and partly through using icons which make them easy to recognize.

Many applications use *palettes*. These are like floating toolbars (though they are rectangular in shape rather than narrow strips) that stay on the screen for as long as you need them. Palettes, can be closed, just like windows, using a button in the top left-hand corner and can, like windows, be moved around by dragging the title bar. Palettes make it easier to organize your screen space to suit your way of working.

Many programs use 'palettes' to make commonly-used tools more accessible. Palettes can be moved around the screen, like windows.

There are subtle but important differences between the way Macs handle windows and how the PC does it. On the PC, document windows have their own menu bars; on the Mac, the menu bar is fixed to the top of the screen, not individual windows. And to close an application on the PC, you simply close the window; on the Mac, the application stays open until you use the 'Quit' menu command.

2.5 Using the Dock

The *Dock* is like a control console for your Mac. It runs along the bottom of the screen and has buttons for launching programs. It's very similar in function to the Taskbar on a Windows PC. When you install a new program on your Mac, its icon will appear here. This means the Dock can eventually become a little overcrowded, but you can clear away icons you don't need simply by dragging them off the Dock, whereupon they disappear in a little puff of smoke. This doesn't mean you can no longer use those applications. They can always be reached via the Applications folder on your hard disk.

The Dock has other icons besides these. At the far left is the **Finder** icon – you can click this to open a new Finder window. The Finder is the Mac's equivalent of Windows Explorer on a PC. You use it to find and organize your files.

Next to the Finder is the **Dashboard** icon. The Dashboard displays the Mac's collection of *widgets*. These are small programs for common basic tasks and include a Calculator, Dictionary and more. There are now thousands of widgets in circulation, and we look at these in more depth in Chapter 15.

Towards the right-hand end of the Dock you will find an icon for the Mac's **System Preferences**. These are equivalent to the Control Panel on a PC, and are used to adjust the display settings, configure different user accounts and more. We look at these in more detail in Chapter 18.

Finally, at the far right of the Dock is the **Trash** icon. This is like the Recycle Bin on a PC. You drag files and folders here when you want to get rid of them, but they don't actually get destroyed until you use the **Empty Trash** menu command, just in case you change your mind.

The latest version of the Mac operating system, *Leopard*, has a slightly different-looking Dock which adds an icon for the new **Time Machine** feature, and separates out a smaller section with two new icons for **Downloads** and **Documents**. We'll examine these more fully in Chapter 4, 'What's new in Leopard'.

2.6   Starting applications

You can start an application by clicking its icon in the Dock, whereupon it will either open the last document you were working on, or a new blank document, or ask you to choose the one you want to open, depending on how that particular program is set up. It's generally quicker, though, to find the document you want to work with in the Finder (see Section 2.7) and double-click it. The Mac knows which application is needed for that document and starts it automatically.

It's quite likely you'll have two or more applications running at the same time as you work, and it's important to know how to switch between them. There are two main ways of doing this. One is to click on a window belonging to the application you want to use (windows are stacked on the screen, and you can often see parts of the window you want underneath the current window), though this does require a little experience. The more reliable method is to look on the Dock for the icon of the application you want to switch to and click on it. That brings the application's open window(s) to the front.

2.7   Using the Finder

Before you can make much progress using different applications on your Mac, though, you need to understand the Finder. This is like any other application, except that it's running all the time the Mac is on and it's really your Mac's control centre. The Finder is what you use to organize your files into folders and to find them again when you need them. If you're already used to how PCs work, think of the Finder as the Mac version of Windows Explorer.

You can create a Finder window by clicking the Finder icon in the Dock. The Finder window contains a *Sidebar* for quick access to common locations and tools, and a window displaying the contents of whatever folder or disk drive you select.

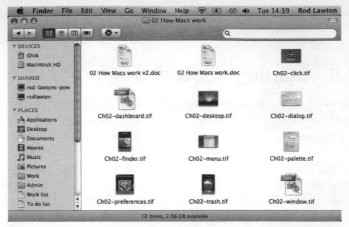

The Finder window is used to examine the contents of your hard disk and its folders. On the left is a Sidebar which offers quick access to common locations.

For example, if you click on the **Macintosh HD** icon in the Sidebar, the window will display the contents of the Mac's hard disk. You can choose the way these are displayed using the buttons running along the top of the Finder window. For example, you can display them as icons, a list, in columns or (new in Leopard) in Cover Flow mode.

Essentially, the Mac contains just two types of object: *files* and *folders*. Folders are simply containers for files or even other folders. You use folders to organize your files in a way that makes sense to you, although the Mac takes charge of some of this organization straight away, with an *Applications* folder and a *System* folder for operating system files you would normally leave well alone.

In Icon view, you can open a folder to see its contents by double-clicking it. The Finder window then displays the contents of that folder. You keep double-clicking as you 'drill down' through your folder system to get to the files you want.

In List view, folders are identified by right-facing arrows. You can click on the arrow to 'expand' the folder and display its contents. This gives you a much clearer picture of the filing system on your Mac, and while it's a little more complicated to take in, most Mac users prefer it to Icon view. List view is very similar to Windows Explorer on the PC.

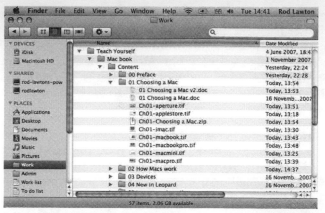

Column view works differently. Here, the Finder window is split vertically into columns. When you click on a folder, its contents are displayed in a column to the right; if you click on a folder in that column, its contents are displayed in another column to the right... and so on. It's a system that makes much more sense when you try it out than it does when someone else is trying to explain it! When you get used to it, you may find that Column view becomes your favourite.

2.8 Your Home folder

The Mac already has a basic filing system in place and it's up to you whether you use this or invent your own. This may depend on whether your Mac is going to be used by other people as well as you. Like PCs, Macs are designed with multiple users in mind. Each user has their own account, which means they have their own login name and a password. Now if you're the only user, you don't have to worry about this. The Mac will start up and run without bothering you with these details. It's only later on, if other family or office members need to use it, that you need to worry about the details of user accounts.

But the by-product of this is that each user has a *Home* on the Mac, even if there is only one user – you. You can see it if you select **Macintosh HD** in the Finder Sidebar and open the *Users* folder. There, you'll see a folder with your username and a little **home** icon. This folder contains a number of other sub-folders for, amongst other things, *Documents*, *Movies*, *Music* and *Pictures*. These folders are where the Mac will store your word processor files, your movie projects, your iTunes songs and your iPhoto library.

Now you can set up your own folder system outside this Home if you want, but then you lose the ability to keep your files separate from other people's. What happens is that if another user has an account on that Mac, they will log on with their own username and password and they will get access only to their *Home* folder and not yours. By keeping your files within the *Home* folder, you also keep them private.

Of course, within the *Documents* folder you can still set up your own folders and subfolders to create a personalized filing system set up specifically for the way you like to work.

Each user on a Mac has their own private 'Home' folder for their documents, photos, music and other files.

rodlawton

2.9 Managing folders and files

To create a new folder, simply open the folder where you want to create it and choose the **New Folder** command from the **File** menu. A new folder is created with the name 'untitled folder' already selected, ready for you to type in the name you want.

You can use the Finder for moving files and folders around, too, and this is generally easier if you open two Finder windows (use the **New Finder Window** command on the **File** menu). First, *navigate* to the folder or file you want to move in one window. Next, use the other window to find the folder you want to move it to. Now just drag the file or folder icon from one window to the other.

To delete a file or folder, just drag its icon on to the **Trash** icon on the toolbar. The Trash isn't emptied straight away, just in case you need to recover items you threw away accidentally. Eventually, though, the Trash will contain so many items that it takes up a significant proportion of your Mac's hard disk space. If you're sure you don't need any of the items in the Trash you can empty it permanently by using the **Empty Trash** command on the **Finder** menu.

The Trash on a Mac is like the Recycle Bin on a PC. You have to empty it from time to time.

2.10 Finding files

It's important to develop a logical filing system and not just leave files and folders lying around haphazardly. It's all too easy to save a file and then forget where you saved it because you weren't paying proper attention or because you couldn't be bothered to navigate to the correct folder in the program's 'Save' dialog.

It's important too to pick file and folder names which are logical and which you'll recognize later. This is second nature to seasoned computer users, but it can take a while to develop this kind of discipline and to work out a system that makes sense to you.

When you do have a logical filing system in place, you'll be able to find any file on your computer straight away, even if you have thousands of them. It's like having a properly-organized filing cabinet in an office.

But for those of us who don't have this kind of discipline, or those occasions when there isn't time to be tidy and methodical about your filing, the Mac can step in with some fast and powerful search tools.

If you take a look at the menu bar (in any application, not just the Finder) you'll see a magnifying glass icon right at the end. You click this to display the Mac's *Spotlight* feature. All you do is type in the name of the file you're looking for and the Mac will search its hard disk to locate it. Spotlight keeps an index of the hard disk's contents which is continually updated, so it can find your files really fast.

Spotlight is the Mac's own search tool. It can find every reference to a word or phrase on your hard disk in moments.

2.11   What if your Mac crashes?

Sometimes Macs crash. It happens to all computers, and even these days to some household appliances. The cause is often impossible to pin down and associated with some freak circumstance deep in the computer's internal processes. Crashes just happen. Usually they're confined to a single program, but they can affect the whole machine. The usual symptom is that the computer freezes. The mouse pointer may keep moving, but the program doesn't respond when you try to click on menus or buttons. You may also see a constantly spinning 'beachball' instead of a pointer – this is the indication that the computer is 'thinking'.

So if a program is frozen, how do you get out of it? There's a special key combination you can use – [Alt]–[Command]–[Esc] (this is just like [Ctrl]–[Alt]–[Delete]) on a PC. This key combination calls up the Mac's **Force Quit** dialog. This lists all the programs currently running and, as often as not, the one that's crashed will be displayed in red. To Force Quit an application, you select it from the list and press the **Force Quit** button at the bottom of the dialog. This will usually solve the problem, though it may be that the whole system has become unstable by now and you need to restart the Mac. You may need to restart to make the rogue application run properly again anyway.

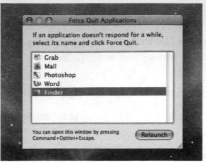

Like all computers, the Mac may crash one day. The Force Quit dialog enables you to close the offending program and carry on working.

2.12 Shutdown and sleep

When you've finished working on your Mac you'll need to switch it off, but to do this you need to use the **Shut Down** command on the **Apple** menu. It's the same with PCs – you can't just disconnect the power.

There is another alternative if you're likely to use the computer again within a few hours, and that is to put it into *sleep* mode instead. Sleep mode switches off the display and the disk drives but maintains the operating system and any applications running in their current state using a small trickle of power. When you 'wake' the Mac again, it's ready to pick up where you left off almost instantly. Apple recommends sleep mode if the Mac's going to be used again within 24 hours, but that you should shut down if it's likely to be longer.

With the MacBook and MacBook Pro laptops, closing the lid will put them into sleep mode, and the internal battery can power the sleep mode for many hours. For example, you could set up a series of documents and presentations in advance of a meeting, close the display, take a train to your client's offices and open up when you get there ready to make your pitch straight away.

Summary

- Macs start up like PCs, by first checking the hardware, then loading the operating system and displaying a Desktop.

- The Finder is used to organize files and folders.

- The Dock displays a list of programs; to start a program, click its icon.

- You can also open files directly by double-clicking them – the Mac starts the appropriate program automatically.

- The Home folder keeps your files separate from everyone else's if your Mac is used by more than one person.

- If you don't know where a file is saved, the Mac's Spotlight tool can find it quickly.

- You can Force Quit an application that's crashed.

- If your Mac is going to be used again soon, you can send it to sleep instead of shutting it down – it will start up again as you left it.

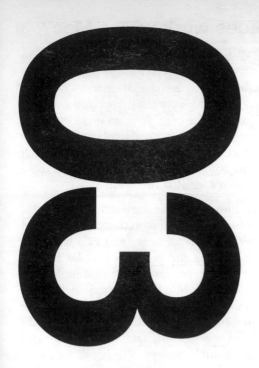

03 plug-in devices

In this chapter you will learn:

- what devices can plug into a Mac
- about USB 1.1, 2.0 and Firewire
- about laser and inkjet printers
- how to scan old photos
- how to transfer photos from a digital camera
- how to connect a camcorder
- about external hard drives and 'stick' drives

3.1 What devices work with a Mac?

While Macs use totally different and incompatible software to PCs, these days they can almost always use the same plug-in devices. These include printers, scanners, digital cameras, memory card readers, camcorders and plug-in hard drives and portable stick drives. This wasn't always the case. In years gone by, Macs used different connectors and were not particularly well supported by makers of devices. You had to make sure that any peripheral you bought was compatible with the Mac, and these might only be available from specialist retailers.

To this day, you may get some computer 'experts' insisting this is one of the failings of the Mac, but this notion is long out of date. When the *USB interface* arrived, Macs and PCs both had the same cable interface, making things much simpler for the makers. And the introduction of the translucent plastic iMac in the 1990s reinvented the Mac as a fun, lifestyle-friendly computer. Today, makers recognize that although Macs still might be in the minority, they represent an important slice of the market which can't be ignored. As a result, it's rare to find a plug-in device which isn't Mac-compatible, and even those whose packaging doesn't carry the 'Mac' icon will often work.

It's always best to check that printers have Mac software, for example, and scanners too, because these rely on special *drivers* which handle the communication between the device and the computer. But other peripherals like digital cameras, external hard disks and 'stick' drives work like generic storage devices. You plug them in, their icon appears on the desktop and you can just treat it like another drive.

Don't worry that you won't be able to find plug-in devices for your Mac, because as a rule just about anything you can plug into a PC will plug into a Mac too. If in doubt, check the box.

3.2 Types of connection

The USB connector has simplified the whole business of connecting peripherals to computers. Macs may come with two USB ports (MacBook), three (iMac), four (Mac Mini) or five (Mac Pro). If this isn't enough, you can connect a USB hub to a single

USB port on the computer – each hub has its own USB ports for connection peripherals – usually four, but sometimes more.

Some devices draw their power from the USB connection, so if you're using a hub, make sure it's one that has its own power supply.

USB devices come in two speeds. The original USB 1.1 standard is quite slow, but there are still some USB 1.1 peripherals around, so do check the specs. The newer USB 2.0 standard is much faster, and this is important for devices which routinely transfer large amounts of data. USB 1.1 is all right for keyboards, mice and printers, but you need USB 2.0 for external hard disks, memory card readers and scanners. All the USB ports on modern Macs are USB 2.0.

But Macs also come with one or more *Firewire* ports. Firewire was used by Macs for high-speed data transfer before USB 2.0 came along, and even now it's still used for some kinds of data transfer, notably for transferring movie footage from camcorders. On the camcorder, it may be called an 'iLink' connection. Firewire comes in two speeds. The original is 'Firewire 400', but there's a newer, faster 'Firewire 800' which is used by a few pro-level devices.

Most Mac owners will only ever use USB 2.0 devices, though, and maybe the Firewire interface occasionally for connecting camcorders.

Macs also sport another interface which looks like a phone cable socket but isn't. This is the *Ethernet* connector, which you use to connect the Mac to a network. But since modern Macs use wireless *Airport* communications, you can also connect to networks without cables (although cable connections are generally a little faster and more reliable).

3.3   Choosing a printer

Generally, the first peripheral most people need is a printer. These come in two main types: laser printers and inkjet printers.

Laser printers use dry *toner* which is applied to the paper using a drum, then sealed into the paper with heat. Laser printers are common in offices because they are cheap to run, require little maintenance and produce printouts which are dry to the touch straight away. It's possible to get colour lasers too, but these are more expensive both to buy and to run. These too are popular in offices for their speed and economy, but they're not suitable for high-quality photographic output.

Inkjet printers use a different technology, squirting tiny droplets of ink on to the paper as the print head moves across the sheet. Inkjet printers are cheaper than lasers and produce much higher quality colour printout. This makes them ideal for home and light office use. The latest models produce superb photo print quality, even those not designed specifically for photo output.

Really, if you're buying a printer for domestic use, an inkjet is the only logical choice. And you don't have to pay much to get a really good one. The cost is actually in the inks, and heavy users will soon notice that replacement ink cartridges are not cheap. This is one of the drawbacks of inkjet printers – that, and the periodic maintenance they require to keep the ink flowing smoothly. This is carried out automatically by the printer at set intervals, but it means even more ink is used up, though printer

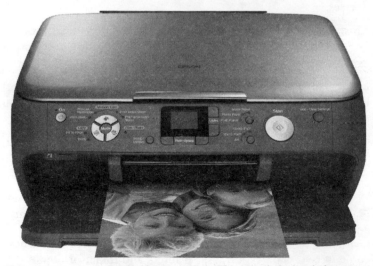

Almost all printers work with Macs as well as PCs – check the box before you buy. An MFD (multi-function device) can scan photos and act as a standalone copier too.

maker HP has introduced recirculating ink systems that return the ink used for maintenance back to the ink tank.

Printers remain popular, but another type of device is slowly taking over – the multi-function device or MFD. MFDs are printers and scanners combined. The scanner sits on the top and you lift the lid then place the items you want to scan face-down on the glass plate (the *platen*).

But because the printer and the scanner are combined, you can bypass the computer altogether if you want to. MFDs usually have a standalone copy feature which means you can copy documents without having to switch the computer on. It's like having a colour photocopier in your own house – very useful for keeping records of correspondence, legal forms or even recipes which you want to pass on.

3.4 Scanning your old photos

Scanners are useful things to have, whether they're standalone devices or built into an MFD. They're especially useful if you have boxes of old prints which you want to digitize on your Mac to preserve them for the future, put them on a web page or repair and enhance them and print them out all over again.

And you don't need a particularly expensive scanner to do this. Most can scan at a level of quality far higher than the things you're scanning.

Resolution is the defining power of the scanner, and it's measured in *DPI* (dots per inch). Typically, even an inexpensive one will have a resolution of 2400dpi, where even a high-quality photographic print is unlikely to have more than 300dpi-worth of detail.

The situation changes if you've got negatives and slides rather than prints. Some scanners have transparency adaptors for scanning these, but the quality of the scans is often disappointing – the pictures don't look as sharp as they should. This is because negatives and slides are tiny and they're being enlarged considerably. The engineering and optical quality of normal scanners just isn't up to the job.

Digital cameras can either be connected to the Mac via a USB cable, or you can take out the memory card and insert it into a card reader to transfer photos.

To get the best definition from slides and negatives you need to use a proper *film* scanner, and these work differently. With a regular scanner, you place the original face-down, flat on the scanning bed. Indeed, they're called *flatbed* scanners. With a film scanner, the slide or negative is fixed in a special holder which is drawn into the scanner during the scanning process. Film scanners are designed specifically for the job, and this shows in the quality of the results.

3.5 Connecting a digital camera

Scanners are perfect for transferring older photos to your computer, but few of us these days shoot with film cameras any more, preferring to use digital cameras instead. Here, of course, there's no need to scan the pictures because they're digital files already. It's still necessary, however, to find some way of transferring them from the camera to the computer, and there are two ways of doing this.

The first is to connect the camera to the computer using the USB cable included with the camera. If you installed the software that came with the camera, this may start up automatically and offer to copy across the photos automatically. Otherwise, you should find that the camera's icon appears on the Desktop, and that you can double-click it to open it and drag the photos across yourself using the Finder.

3.6   Using a memory card reader

For many people, a memory card reader will be more convenient than connecting the camera to the computer by cable. Here,
you take the memory card out of the camera and plug it into a
slot on the card reader (the card reader is connected to the computer). The memory card will appear on the Mac's Desktop and
you can double-click it to open it in the Finder and copy files
across.

Of course, what complicates things with memory cards is that
there are a number of different formats. *SD* cards are the most
common, and are found in the majority of compact digital cameras and some of the cheaper digital SLRs. *Compact Flash* cards
are larger, and although they were once the most popular type,
they're now found mainly in professional digital cameras.

These are the two most common types, though Olympus and
Fujifilm cameras use tiny *xD* cards, while the Sony cameras use
proprietary *Memory Sticks*.

This means you need to check you're buying the right kind of
card reader for your camera's memory cards. The alternative is
to buy a card reader with slots for all the main formats. These
don't necessarily cost much more, and they give you more flexibility in the future if you decide to change camera.

3.7   Movies from your camcorder

Compact digital cameras can also shoot short movie clips, and
these are great for informal video snapshots and they're great
for those bitten by the YouTube bug. However, serious video
fans will use dedicated camcorders, and while an increasing
number of these have solid state storage (high-capacity memory
cards or built-in hard disks), the majority still use tapes.

Now you may be happy just to play back your tapes via a cable
and your domestic TV set. But many video fans want to do a
little work on their movies first, cutting and editing clips, splic-
ing them digitally and adding professional-looking transitions,
fades, titles and credits.

That's exactly what iMovie is for. We won't get into a detailed explanation of what iMovie does here because it's covered more fully in Chapter 11. However, we will explain how the movies get from the camcorder to the computer. It's done via the Firewire, or *iLink* connector on the camcorder and the Firewire port on the Mac. You can use iMovie, which comes with all Macs as part of the iLife suite, to control the camera playback from the computer, stopping and starting the tape, and recording clips to the Mac's hard disk.

Apple does publish a list of camcorders which are officially compatible with iMovie on its website, but in practice there are many more which are not on that list which work fine. Indeed, any camcorder with a Firewire/iLink interface should just plug in and go.

Most plug-in devices connect via a USB socket, but MiniDV digital camcorders use Firewire. All Macs come with Firewire ports too.

3.8   Why external hard drives are useful

Printers, scanners, cameras and camcorders are probably the most obviously useful Mac accessories, but you should also consider investing in an external hard disk drive. Not the most glamorous of peripherals, to be sure, but one that's both practical and, occasionally, an absolute life-saver.

External hard drives come in different capacities and sizes. The largest will sit on your desk alongside your Mac and have their own power adaptor. They offer big capacities (500Gb, or even 1000Gb), but they're not portable.

Portable hard drives have smaller capacities (up to 250Gb currently), but apart from being smaller, they run on the power provided by the USB cable – they don't need a power cable at all. Portable drives are useful for all kinds of things. You can use them to boost the capacity of a MacBook (the hard drives in the Mac laptops soon fill up), you can use them for transporting large movie files or photo collections from one computer to another, and you can use them for possibly the most important function of all – backups.

Computer experts are always telling us to back up our important files, and they're right. Hard disks don't fail often, but they do fail. So just sit and think for a minute of the consequences of losing forever all the data on your computer – awful, isn't it?

This is an external hard disk drive. It plugs into a USB socket on the Mac and gets all its power from that too. You can use it for transporting data or backups.

Backups are vital and, with a portable hard disk, easy to manage. Those who subscribe to a .Mac account (see Chapter 14) get an Apple utility called *Backup* which makes it easy. Alternatively, if you're using Leopard (see Chapter 4), Time Machine will take care of it.

The portability is an important factor. It's all very well having a static hard disk drive plugged into your computer, but if the computer is stolen or damaged in a fire, you can expect to lose your backup too. But with a portable drive, you can get into the routine of keeping it at a different location to your computer, and this is a key feature of any kind of backup strategy.

3.9 Portable stick drives

In the old days, the standard way of transferring files between computers was the floppy disk. It's been a long time since any Mac came equipped with a floppy disk drive, so how's it done now?

Usually, files these days are swapped over the Internet as email attachments or, for those working in an office, transferred over the office network. Sometimes, though, a simpler method is needed – when students need to take an assignment into class, maybe, or when amateur photographers want to take digital photos into a camera club meeting.

One way of doing this is to *burn* a CD. All modern Macs have built-in CD writers, and it's a comparatively simple process: you insert a blank CD, copy the files across to its icon and then burn it. This is a once-only process that writes the files permanently to the CD.

This takes a few moments to do, though, and it does seem quite wasteful, especially if the CD isn't filled, and if it's only being used for data transfer rather than permanent storage.

It's much better to use a solid-state stick drive, and these are widely available in computer and electronics stores. They have several advantages. For a start, they're quick and convenient to use. You plug them into a USB port on the Mac, their icon appears on the desktop and you can just copy across the files you

'Stick' drives are perfect for transporting large files. They're tiny enough to fit on a keyring, but available in capacities up to a staggering 8Gb.

want to transfer using the Finder. They're also reusable – you can delete the information and copy across new files as many times as you like. They're very small and easy to carry around and can even be attached to keyrings. They're robust, there is no risk of physical scratches or marks affecting the data and nowadays they're pretty inexpensive, too. A 1Gb stick drive holds almost twice as much data as a CD, and you can get them in 2Gb, 4Gb and even 8Gb capacities too.

These stick drives have become the new floppy!

3.10   Keyboards and mice

Lastly, although most Macs are supplied with a keyboard and mouse, these are also available separately. This is especially relevant for the Mac Mini, which Apple has described as the 'BYODKM' computer (Bring Your Own Display, Keyboard and Mouse). The Mac Mini is designed as a taster for PC owners who want to try out a Mac without buying a whole system – you unhook the PC from these components and hook up the Mac Mini instead.

That's an extreme example, but there could be instances where you want to use a different keyboard, mouse or display with your Mac. These don't have to be Mac-specific. PC keyboards will work fine, though they do have to have a USB connection rather than the PS2 type (it may also be necessary to re-map certain control keys using the Mac's System Preferences). PC mice work fine, just as they are, even those with scroll wheels, and you can plug in a PC's display, too, though if it's an analogue rather than a digital display, you will need an adaptor for the Mac, which only has a digital connector.

Laptop users often prefer to use a plug-in USB keyboard rather than the built-in keyboards when they can because the keys are generally better. And a proper mouse is certainly preferable to a trackpad.

Apple's Wireless Mighty Mouse is one of the best, though also one of the most expensive at £50 in the UK. It uses the built-in Bluetooth capability of all current Macs to work without cables, and it has a unique scrollball in the top which not only scrolls vertically but sideways too (depending on the program you're using it with).

Not all devices connect by cable. Apple's Mighty Mouse uses a wireless Bluetooth connection, and it's possible to swap data with some mobile phones this way, too.

All this should serve to emphasize the point made at the beginning of this chapter. These days the Mac is a mainstream computer that's catered for by nearly all peripherals makers as a matter of course, and this includes printers, scanners, cameras, disk drives and just about any other gadget you might want to get. If in doubt, just check the box for the 'Mac' icon or read the system requirements to see if the Mac is mentioned.

Note that this applies to hardware devices only and NOT to software!

Summary

- Nowadays, most plug-in devices work with both Macs and PCs.

- USB 2.0 is much faster at transferring data than the old USB 1.1.

- Macs also come with Firewire connectors, but these are not often needed.

- Laser printers are good for the office, inkjets are better for home use.

- Multi-function devices combine a printer and a scanner, and can be used for standalone copying.

- Flatbed scanners are fine for prints, but for best quality from negatives you need a film scanner.

- A memory card reader is often more convenient for transferring photos from your digital camera than connecting it by cable.

- You can transfer camcorder footage straight into iMovie using a Firewire (iLink) cable.

- External hard disks are ideal for extra storage, transporting data and regular backups.

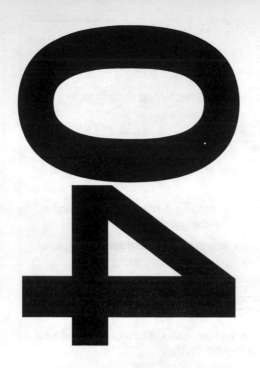

04 what's new in Leopard

In this chapter you will learn:

- about Leopard and Tiger
- how Stacks work
- about Cover Flow and Quick Look
- how Smart Folders can find files
- how Spaces can help you work on many things at once
- how Time Machine can back up your data automatically
- about the changes to the email, browsing and chat programs

4.1 Do you need to upgrade?

Leopard, or OS X 10.5 to give it its technical name, is the latest version of the Mac operating system, and it replaces OS X 10.4 *Tiger* in much the same way that Windows Vista superseded Windows XP.

However, the jump between Tiger and Leopard isn't as great, and while many existing Mac owners will be wondering whether they should upgrade, there really is no hurry. If you buy a new Mac now, it will come with Leopard as standard.

A great deal of work has been done to the Mac operating system at a low level, behind the scenes, but for most people the differences are cosmetic and related to everyday tools and procedures. Leopard does look subtly different to Tiger, and there are many new features in Leopard that are genuinely useful. However, upgrading is by no means essential. Tiger remains a thoroughly modern, up-to-date operating system with life in it yet – much more so than Windows XP following the arrival of Vista.

Some of the enhancements in Leopard apply to Safari, Mail and other Apple programs included as standard with Macs, but most apply to the Finder, and these are what we'll be looking at in this chapter.

Mac OS X 10.5 Leopard is now pre-installed on all new Macs, but can be bought separately as an upgrade for those running Tiger (photo: courtesy of Apple).

4.2 Stacks

First, off, you'll notice that the Dock in Leopard not only has a new translucent look, but that there's a new section over on the far right. This is where you'll find a new feature called *Stacks*. Stacks open in a fan shape to show you their contents. By default, there's a *Downloads* Stack which opens to show recently downloaded files. These are files you may have clicked on a web page, or files which have been sent to you as email attachments which you save. When there are too many files to display in a Stack, it changes to show them in a window as a grid instead.

But you can also add your own folders to this area of the Dock simply by dragging them on to the Dock from the Finder. For example, you can drag the *Applications* folder here, or your *Documents* folder.

The Stacks feature does have a weakness, though. It's no use for accessing folders within folders, and many applications do indeed install into subfolders within the *Applications* folder. This applies even more to the *Documents* folder, where you'll almost certainly store your work in subfolders, so Stacks don't really help you much there.

You may find Stacks very useful, but it's equally likely that you'll find them a novelty and not much more, especially if you're used to Macs already and you've managed perfectly well without them until now.

Stacks can be used to show the contents of favourite folders as a fan. It looks clever, but its value is less certain – it's not much use if any of the contents are in subfolders.

4.3 Cover Flow

Cover Flow is a new way to view the contents of folders in addition to the existing Icon, List and Column views. Anyone who's used the latest version of iTunes on a Mac may already have seen Cover Flow in action – visually, it's like flicking through a stack of CD covers. Now that idea's been extended to the Finder, so that you can flick through a folder full of photos, for example, seeing each one move to the foreground as you drag the scrollbar underneath from left to right.

This is certainly a new way to browse through your files visually – something that's been lacking in the Mac OS until now. For those new to the Mac it's both novel and rather clever. For those who've been using Macs for a while, it may be less appealing because it is as much a cosmetic benefit as a practical one.

It's possible too that Apple is simply introducing consistency across its range of applications and devices. Both iTunes and the iPhone rely on Cover Flow, so it might look odd if the Mac OS didn't offer it too.

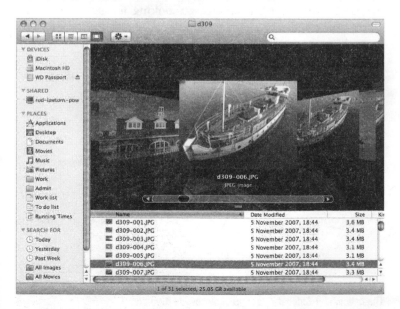

Cover Flow is a new way to look at the contents of your folders. You can flick through your files, which are shown as large preview images.

4.4 Finder Sidebar

The Finder Sidebar has changed from that in Tiger. It still offers quick access to items on your Mac, but the layout and functions are different.

In Tiger, the Sidebar was split into two sections. The top section listed Volumes attached to the Mac, including its hard disk(s), iDisk (for those with a .Mac account) and any computers currently connected via a network. In the bottom part were shortcuts to many locations on the hard disk, including standard items like the Desktop, the Applications folder, Documents, Movies, Music and Pictures. You were also able to add your own items to the bottom of the list simply by dragging files or folders on to the Sidebar from the Finder.

Leopard's Sidebar has more sections. These are: Devices, Shared, Places, Search For. Devices is like the top section in the old Sidebar, listing any disk drives built into or connected to the Mac. Any networked machines are now split off from this list and displayed in the Places section underneath. Note that with Leopard you no longer have to go looking for networked machines to connect to them manually – Leopard automatically scans for other machines on the network and lists them here. The Places section corresponds to the lower section in the Tiger Sidebar. Here you'll find Applications, Desktop, Document and so on as before, together with any items you drag on to the Sidebar yourself.

This all sounds quite complicated, but to start with, just think of the Sidebar as a set of shortcuts to useful things on your Mac.

The Search For section is new, though, and includes a brand new Leopard feature called *Smart Folders*.

The new Finder Sidebar offers quick access to items on your hard disk, any plug-in disk drives and other computers on the network.

4.5 Smart Folders

If you've spent any time in iPhoto you may already know how Smart Albums work, and Smart Folders work on the same principle. You can think of them as saved searches. Let's imagine your hard disk is getting filled up by large image files. With a Smart Folder it'll be easy enough to track them down:

1 Open the **File** menu and choose **New Smart Folder**. A search window opens with a search bar prompting you to choose between searching the whole Mac or just your home folder, and between searching file contents or filenames. We want to search the whole Mac, but we don't need to search the contents because we're not looking for text information.

2 Now we need to add our search criteria by clicking the '+' button at the far right of the search bar. This adds another bar with buttons for **Kind** and **Any**. Both of these are actually pop-up menus with different values, but we can leave **Kind** as it is and just open the **Any** menu. From this list we choose **Images**. Now our Smart Folder is locating all the Image files on our Mac.

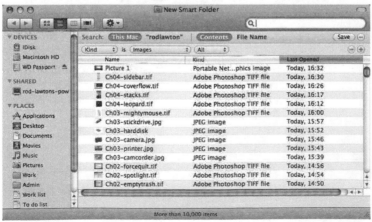

3 This can now be refined. First, because of the options we've chosen a third button appears on the search bar – **All**. This means the Smart Folder will find all images of all types. If we want to, we can choose a specific type from this menu, for example JPEG or TIFF. What we're more interested in, though, is the file size, so we'll leave this set to **All**.

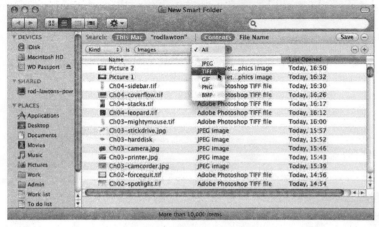

4 To look for specific file sizes, we need another search criterion, and we can create one by clicking the '+' button at the end of the search bar again. This time, from the first pop-up menu we choose **Size**. (If this doesn't appear on the list, click the **Other** option at the bottom.)

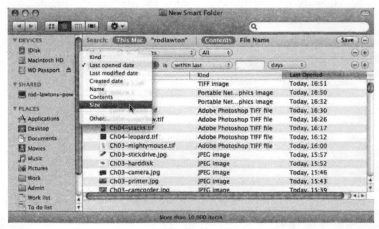

5 In the next pop-up to the right we choose 'greater than', and in the box to the right of this we can type a number for the file size. Let's say we want to find files bigger than 10Mb. We type '10' in this box and make sure the pop-up to the right of this is set to 'Mb'.

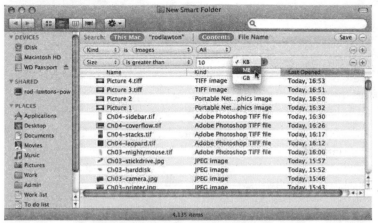

6 As you choose the search options, the window below fills up with a list of matching files – the list will grow shorter as you refine the search criteria. You can check this list to make sure the search is finding the files you meant it to and, if it is, click the **Save** button at the top right to choose a name for your new Smart Search and to save it. It will now appear at the bottom of the **Search For** section of the Sidebar, ready to be used any time you need to perform a clean-out of your big image files.

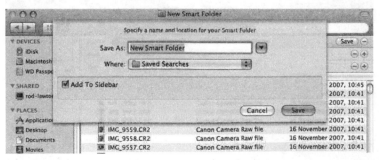

4.6 Quick Look

For a while Windows has scored over the Mac OS in its ability to display documents, particularly photos, as thumbnail images. You can open a folder full of photos and see what they are without having to rely solely on their filename to identify them.

Leopard puts that right with a feature called *Quick Look*, which works alongside Cover Flow in giving a visual representation of each file. In Leopard, when you view folder contents as icons, or use Cover Flow, files are displayed as thumbnail images showing the actual file contents. Leopard supports many file types, including Microsoft Office documents, PDF files and more.

But with Cover Flow, you're not limited to these previews. If you select a file in the Finder and hit the spacebar, Leopard displays a large-size preview in a pop-up window. Still not big enough? Then click the **Full Screen** button. When you've seen enough, you click the **X** button to close the window.

With the new Quick Look feature, you can examine many different types of file without having to open them in an application.

4.7 Spaces

Leopard makes it easy to view the contents of individual files without opening them, which is a real time-saver. But it also offers new ways to manage your windows and make the most of your screen space. It's called *Spaces*, and it's like being able to switch between four (or more) different monitors, depending on what you want to work on.

1 To activate Spaces you have to open the System Preferences and choose **Expose & Spaces**. Select the **Spaces** tab and check the **Enable Spaces** box. By default, there are four Spaces, but you can add more if you think you'll need them. At the bottom of the dialog is a list of the keyboard shortcuts you need – [F8] to display the Spaces, and arrow and number keys to move between them.

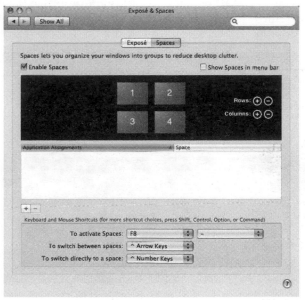

2 When you close the System Preferences, you'll be back where you were on the Mac, but with a difference. Now, when you hit [F8] a grid will pop-up showing the Spaces currently running. At the moment, only the top left space will have anything in it. If you click one of the others you'll get a blank Desktop as if you had no programs running at all.

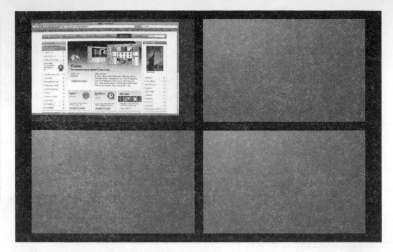

3 You can now start opening files and applications in this Space, and return to the first one at any time by pressing [F8] and selecting it.

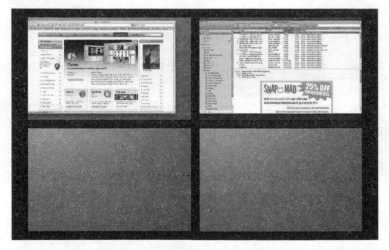

So what's the point? Let's imagine you're doing several things at once throughout the day (as most of us are). You can start Mail, Safari and iCal in one Space to handle your everyday admin, start up Pages and Keynote in another to work on a report or a business presentation, and start up iPhoto in a third Space to sort through your latest batch of digital photos when you take a coffee break from work.

Now running all these applications at once, in a single Space, will make your desktop very cluttered. But by splitting them into different Spaces you give yourself a much cleaner, less cluttered working environment that can be organized according to the activity you're carrying out at any one time. You can also use Spaces to work on more than one project at once, and have Mail, Safari, iCal and so on open in both of them. The possibilities are, as they say, endless.

4.8 Time Machine

Time Machine is one of Leopard's most impressive and most ambitious features. It's a tool for backing up the entire contents of your hard disk, automatically, in the background, for ever.

At a recent Leopard presentation, Apple revealed results of a survey they had conducted into backups. Over 90% of those they questioned said they considered backups vital, but only 4% of them actually did back up their files.

Traditionally, backup software has been time-consuming, technical and tricky to use, and Time Machine aims to sweep all this aside with a solution so simple that there's now no excuse for not backing up.

First, you need to invest in an external disk drive larger than the one in the Mac – preferably, several times larger. That's not as outlandish as it sounds because external USB hard disks are inexpensive these days, and a 500Gb drive will cost less than £100 in the UK, and a 1000Mb (terabyte) drive as little as £150.

The first time you plug in a new external drive, Leopard will ask you if you want to use it for Time Machine. It's best to use one drive specifically for this alone. Leopard will then perform a full backup, which will take some time, but will happen in the background, so you can get on with your work. Once this full backup has been made, Time Machine will carry out regular *incremental* backups, backing up only those things which have changed since last time.

If you need to restore your whole Mac to an earlier state, you can now restore that state with Time Machine, going back in

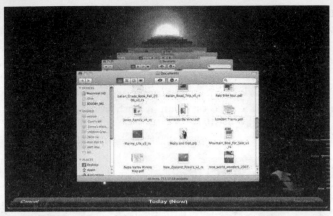

Apple describes Time Machine rather amusingly as 'a giant step backwards'. It's Leopard's innovative new backup tool.

time through its backups to find the state you want. You can also restore individual files and folders in the same way.

Eventually, this external drive will fill up because Time Machine is adding more and more backups all the time. So what do you do then? Apple's suggestion is simple. Disconnect the drive, put it somewhere safe, get another drive and start again. It might not be the cheapest solution, but it's by far the simplest and most practical.

• For best security, you should unplug your external hard drive and store it away from your Mac between sessions.

4.9 Boot Camp

Boot Camp is not brand new, but this is the first version of the Mac OS where it's been included as standard (previously it was an unfinished beta version which had to be downloaded from the Apple website). Boot Camp takes advantage of the fact that modern Macs use the same Intel processor family as Windows PCs and that, technically, there's no reason why Macs shouldn't run Windows.

Boot Camp enables the Mac to start as a PC, but it's important to understand that you will have to buy and install your own copy of Windows – Windows is not included with Boot Camp.

You will also have to set up a separate disk partition for Windows to run in. The Boot Camp Assistant walks you through the whole process, and from this point on you can start your Mac up as a PC or a Mac, whichever you choose.

What you can't do, though, is run both at the same time (though there are utilities around to do this). But it does mean you can switch to PC mode for those occasions where you just don't have the software you need on the Mac.

4.10 Application enhancements

In addition to the changes to Finder, there are enhancements to many of the Apple programs that come with Leopard. The key ones are summarized here.

Mail

Mail, the Mac's email program, has been upgraded with several new features. You can now set up *Smart Mailboxes* which work like Smart Folders in the Finder – once you've set up the search criteria, these mailboxes automatically display messages which match them. For example, you could have a Smart Mailbox set up to display messages containing any mention of your favourite soccer team.

And when you receive a message from someone who includes their telephone number and/or address, Mail will spot it and display a pop-up menu alongside which enables you to add the person to your Address Book as a new contact or amend the existing details if they're in it already.

There are 30 *stationery* templates now to make your messages look much more attractive and interesting. Perhaps the most useful additions, though, are the *Notes* and *To Do* features. Now, within Mail, you can jot down a telephone number, travel directions or any other information as a note and these appear in the *Reminders* section of Mail's new Sidebar.

It's the same with To Dos. According to Apple, many users send themselves emails as reminders, so it made sense to incorporate this into Mail properly. The cleverest part is that these To Dos integrate with iCal, so that jobs you add in iCal also appear in Mail and vice versa.

Apple Mail now includes To Dos, Notes and Smart Mailboxes which can gather mail about specific subjects automatically.

Safari

Safari is the Mac's web browser and it's received some subtle but useful enhancements in Leopard. Previously, the ability to open many web pages in tabs in the same window was one of Safari's top features, but now these tabs can be re-organized into a different order, turned into a new window or, if your screen is cluttered up with enough Safari windows already, you can combine them into a single window with multiple tabs. (For more on this, see Section 5.6.)

Other improvements include a new Find function which opens a special **Find** bar at the top of the window. (This is not the same as searching the Web using a site like Google – it's for searching the text in the current web page.) When you search for a word or phrase, the Search bar tells you how many matches have been found and lets you go through them one by one using arrow

Safari has a new Find tool which tells you how many matches it finds on a page and even highlights them for you.

buttons. The web page itself is dimmed out and the found items are highlighted so that you can easily see where they are. It's a huge improvement on traditional web page Find functions.

iChat

If you're an Internet chat fan you'll be interested in the new features in the Mac's iChat application. It can be used as a text-only chat tool, but it really comes into its own when both you and your chat buddies are using computers with webcams (these are built into the screen on many Mac models).

Some of the enhancements are purely cosmetic, like the ability to use a photo backdrop so that it looks as though you are standing in front of the Eiffel Tower or Niagara Falls or wherever, and the selection of weird distortions and other photo effects you can now apply to your video image.

The cleverest thing, though, is the way you can show your chat buddies keynote presentations (for example) live. In fact, this can be done with a wide range of applications. Your video image shrinks down to a corner of the screen, but you can still keep up a video commentary on what you're showing on the screen. It's really quite remarkable to be able to do this, and simple to set up, too.

For those who use chat programs, the new iChat is a revelation, thanks to its new theatre mode which lets you show other people, things on your computer.

Summary

* Many of the changes in Leopard are cosmetic, but worthwhile nonetheless.

* Smart Folders can automatically find specific files, wherever they are, and display them in a single place.

* Time Machine is the simplest backup solution yet and the first to be built into an operating system as standard.

* With Boot Camp and a copy of Windows, you can start up your Mac as a PC, though the initial setup is somewhat technical.

* The Mac's email, browsing and chat programs have all been improved and Mail now offers Notes and To Dos.

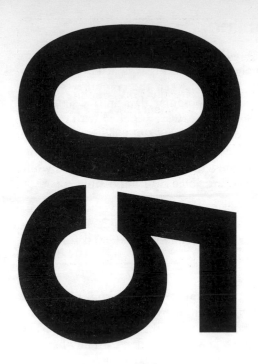

05

Internet and email

In this chapter you will learn:

- how dial-up and broadband connections differ
- about routers and modems
- how to surf the Internet
- how to use bookmarks
- how to shop online
- about tabbed browsing
- how to set up an email account
- how to send and receive mail
- what to do with 'junk'

5.1 Getting online

To use the Internet and email with your Mac, you will need an Internet connection. In the old days this was achieved using a *modem*, a device which fitted between the computer and the phone line and converted the computer data into a signal the phone line could carry. Some Macs were supplied with modems built in. However, these dial-up connections via modems and regular phone lines are slow and impractical for the way the Internet is used today. Besides, they tie up the phone line while the computer is online, making voice calls impossible.

The modern way to connect to the Internet is via an *ADSL* or *broadband* connection. This has many advantages, including much faster data transfer rates, which are essential for things like video chat, downloading music or watching video clips on YouTube.

To use broadband in the UK you must first get your phone line converted. This is usually organized by the company you buy your broadband service from as part of the overall package. The work is done at the local exchange – you don't usually have an engineer calling at your house – and typically takes a few days.

You then need a device for connecting your computer to the phone line. This may be a *broadband modem*. These are often supplied free as part of your broadband subscription. Their disadvantage is that they can only connect one computer to the Internet.

The other option is a *router*. A router is a device designed to connect two or more computers to form a network, but many also incorporate a broadband modem. If you only have one computer, they work just like a broadband modem. But if you have two or more computers, you can connect each to this single router, and they will all be able to access the Internet through it. It will also be possible to swap files between these computers because they are now on a network.

A broadband router (also called an *ADSL router* or *modem router*) is the best way to connect to the Internet because it's the most flexible. And if you buy a *wireless* router, you will not need to connect your Mac to it with a cable. All new Macs come with

Airport wireless networking as standard, so you will be able to use them to connect to the Internet anywhere in the house as long as it's within the router's wireless range.

Most broadband accounts come with a modem, but it's worth upgrading to a router, which can connect several computers to each other and the Internet.

Setting up your connection

There are two ways of setting up an Internet connection, depending on whether you're using a modem or a router. The company supplying your broadband connection will supply you with all the technical details needed to configure your connection, though these will only apply to any modem or router supplied by them. If you buy a router separately, you will need to use the same information in conjunction with the router's own manual.

Some broadband companies will supply instructions specifically for Mac users, though many assume you have a PC. If you're having any difficulties with the setup, try the Mac's *Network Setup Assistant*. You can find this by opening the System Preferences using the icon on the Dock and then clicking the **Network** button. At the bottom of the Network dialog is an **Assist me** button which launches the Assistant. This walks you through the configuration process step-by-step, and this is where you'll need the account and setup information provided by your broadband company.

If you're setting up a router, the process is slightly different. With a modem, it's the Mac that handles all the setup information. With a router, you program this into the router itself. The router instructions will tell you how to apply the settings, and many offer a wizard which walks you through the process step-by-step. Again, this is where you'll need the account information from your broadband company.

Setting up Internet accounts isn't at all difficult, but if you've not done it before it can be confusing. With this in mind, you might want to choose a broadband provider which supports Mac owners as well as PC owners.

It's not the most cost-effective solution, but if your broadband supplier provides a modem, you can get started with that and then invest in a router later on to get the advantage of networking and wireless connections.

Your Internet provider will give you the information you need to configure your modem or router.

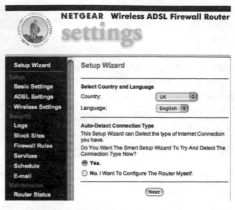

Working away from home

One big advantage of wireless networking is that you can more easily work away from home. It's not always possible to find a convenient wireless *hotspot*, but it's becoming easier. For example, if you're visiting a business colleague or customer, they may have wireless access points within the office or the building that you can use directly, although some will require authorization in the form of a username and a password, for example. Friends and relatives will often have their own wireless routers too, and the Mac will identify these automatically and ask if you want to use them to connect to the Internet. If you're staying in a big hotel you'll usually find that Internet access is available, but that it's password-protected and there's a charge for using it. Smaller hotels, though, may have much less formal arrangements and may not make any charge for using their wireless connection. Just ask at the reception desk to find out. Some cafes offer Internet access, but again you have to pay a charge to use them, and you'll be on your third espresso by the time you've got past the registration screens. It may also be possible to pick up a stray wireless connection in the street, but it's very unwise to use networks you find without asking permission because it's a criminal offence to steal bandwidth from other people's networks in these circumstances, and arrests have been made on this basis.

5.2 Getting started with Safari

Once your Internet connection is configured, when you start Safari, it will connect to the Internet automatically. With old-fashioned dial-up connections, this might take 30 seconds or more, but today's broadband accounts are *always on*, so you should be online in seconds.

Safari will now load your *home page*. By default, this will be the Apple website, but you can change this to whatever you like by choosing **Preferences** from the **Safari** menu. In the **General** tab you will see a box for the **Home page**. Type in the address of the page you would like as your home page here.

There are three main ways of going to web pages in Safari. One is to follow links on other pages, another is to type the address of the web page into the Address Bar running along the top of the window, and a third way is to use a *bookmark* you've saved previously.

5.3 Using bookmarks

Web addresses can be hard to remember and time-consuming to type in, so bookmarks are the easy way to store the locations of your favourite sites.

To create a bookmark:

1 Go to the page you want and choose **Add Bookmark** from the **Bookmarks** menu.

2 A dialog will pop up where you can choose a name for the bookmark and where you want to save it.

3 By default, Safari will display the web page title chosen by its designer, but you will often find it useful to type in something shorter and easier to recognize later.

4 As to where you save the bookmark, there are three choices. You can save it in the main bookmark list with no attempt at organization, you can save it in a bookmark folder (depending on whether you have any set up yet), or you can save it in the Bookmark Bar, which runs horizontally across the top of the screen. This bar should be kept for the pages you view most often, though, because the space available is limited.

To view your bookmarks:

1 Click the **Show all bookmarks** button at the far left-hand end of the Bookmarks Bar.

2 If you're using Tiger you'll see a Sidebar on the left containing a list of **Collections** (sets of bookmarks), and clicking on any of these will display the collection's contents in the main window to the right.

◆ In Leopard, the Sidebar is split into **Collections** and individual **Bookmarks** but the items themselves are the same.

3 Using this window you can create new folders for organizing your bookmarks, and you can also choose which bookmarks will be visible directly in the **Bookmarks** menu by dragging them to the *Bookmarks Menu* collection. You can also change what's displayed in the *Bookmarks Bar* collection, and hence the Bookmarks Bar itself.

4 To visit any of the web pages in your list of bookmarks, just double-click it.

5.4 Searching online

The Web, as we're constantly being reminded, contains an almost unimaginable wealth of information on any topic you could possibly think of. This is where you need to use a *search engine*. These search the whole Web for the words or phrases you enter in the *search field* and come back with a list of websites containing them. The trouble is that these may run to tens of thousands, and there is an awful lot of dross and irrelevant information out there which you need to sift through to find what you want. After a while you develop an eye for the sites which are going to be reliable and offer the most useful information, but it helps to use a good search engine in the first place, because the smarter ones can identify the most relevant sites and put them at the top of the list.

One of the best-known search engines today is Google. It's now so prominent that Safari includes a Google search box in the top right-hand corner of the toolbar:

1 First, type the word or phrase you're looking for onto the search box and press the [**Return**] key.

2 Google will come back with a list of sites, together with an extract to help you identify those which may be most useful.

3 To view a website, just click on its title in the list of search results. Better still, **[Command]**-click it to open it in a new tab so that your search results remain accessible.

Google is not the only search engine you can use, though. For example, you could try **uk.ask.com**, or **uk.yahoo.com**. All you need to do is type the address into Safari's Address Bar to go to the site.

5.5 Buying online

It's now possible to buy many items on the Web at lower prices than you could find elsewhere, and there are many more things you can buy online which are simply not available in ordinary stores.

Buying online may seem a little daunting at first because you're dealing with a machine and not a real person, and the transaction doesn't feel quite as concrete. You may also have heard scare stories about Internet fraud and goods which fail to arrive.

In reality, the risks are no greater than ordering by telephone or from a mail order catalogue. Think of it this way: when you order via a website you're telling a computer what you want; when you order by telephone, you're telling a human operator who's probably typing it into exactly the same computer...

It is best to stick to well-known brands or companies, especially those you've seen advertised in magazines or which you've been told about by friends. One very good example is www.amazon.co.uk, which sells books, DVDs, photographic equipment and more. A few years ago, comparatively few people had heard of Amazon and fewer still used it regularly. Now, it's one of the best-known online stores.

Online transactions are quite straightforward, and you get confirmation in writing straight away by email or via your web browser, which you don't get when ordering goods by phone.

Typically, this is how it works:

1 If it's the first time you've bought from this particular company, you'll usually be asked to create a personal account, with your own username and password so that no one else has access to it.

2 Next, you browse the site for the items you want and add them to a virtual shopping trolley or basket.

3 When you've finished shopping you go to the *checkout* page, where you can check and confirm the contents of your basket. You'll be shown a total cost, plus any postage or packing charges.

4 The payment process usually takes place over a series of screens, step-by-step. You'll be asked for the details of the card which you're going to pay with, and then the address you want the goods delivered to. This must usually be the cardholder's home address – the card company may refuse to authorize the payment where delivery is to a different address.

5 Finally, you complete the checkout process and confirm your order. You'll have been asked for your email address at some point in the registration/checkout process, and confirmation of the order will now be sent to you. This is your permanent record of the transaction, and you can print it out if you wish, but it's stored on your computer anyway. Some websites may display the order confirmation as a web page instead,

and you should print this out in the absence of any email confirmation.

6   Your goods will now be delivered by post, just as if you'd ordered by phone or from a catalogue.

Buying online is easy, and can often be less error-prone than doing it by phone. There are many big names now, including www.amazon.co.uk

5.6   Working with tabs

Sometimes it's useful to have more than one web page open at a time, and there are two ways of doing this. One is to open up the new web page in a new window, and you can do this by using the **New Window** command on the **File** menu and typing the address into the new Safari window's Address Bar.

Alternatively, if you're following a link from an existing page, you can hold down [Ctrl] as you click on the link. This displays a pop-up shortcut menu, and the first two options are **Open Link in New Window** and **Open Link in New Tab**.

When you use this second option, Safari creates a new tab within the current window, and loads that page into it. You can see all

See the row of tabs running across below the menu bar? Each one marks a different web page. Click the tab to view the page.

the open tabs in a horizontal bar which appears below the Bookmarks Bar. (If you're using Tiger and you don't see any tabs, open the Safari Preferences, go to the Tabs section and make sure **Enable Tabbed Browsing** is switched on.)

There's an even quicker way to open links in new tabs – just hold down [Command] as you click the link.

Tabs are a great way to browse through lots of linked pages because you don't fill up your screen with lots of separate windows, and you can keep the page you started from open, which means you're less likely to get lost on the Internet.

5.7 Getting starting with Mail

Once your Internet connection is working there's nothing else you need to do in order to be able to surf the Web. With email, it's different. The Internet connection is only half the story – you also have to set up your email account(s) in Mail.

You normally get an email account as part of your broadband package, but it's also possible to set up free email accounts separately with Yahoo! and other providers.

To set up an email account:

1 Choose **Preferences** from the **Mail** menu and then click the **Accounts** button. This window will show you the email accounts currently set up, if any, and in the bottom left-hand corner is a '+' button for adding a new one.

2 Press this. Mail will start a step-by-step guide to adding an account, and for this you will need certain information from the company providing the email account.

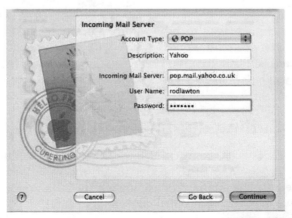

3 First, you type in your name, your email address and your password. The email address and password will have been given to you when you set up the account.

4 Next, in the **Incoming Mail Server** window, choose the account type from a menu. Most are *POP* accounts. This means the emails are downloaded from a computer called a POP server to your Mac. In this same window you need to type in a **Description** of your account (just so that you can recognize it from a list if necessary), the **Incoming Mail Server**, **User Name** and **Password**. This information will be provided by the email service provider. At this point, Mail will check this connection is working.

5 Next, specify the **Outgoing Mail Server**. Here, you should use the outgoing mail server specified by your broadband company. If you set up an email account with another provider, they may give you a different address to type in, but this probably won't work. Broadband providers are prickly about letting you sending mail through any other server than their own (we must presume there's a good technical reason for this). Don't check the **Use Authentication** box unless your email provider's told you to. Mail will now check this connection and, if all's well, you've successfully set up your email account.

Normally, email messages are stored on the mail server (or POP server) until you connect and download them to your computer. Similarly, any messages you write are stored on your computer until you send them. This is all very well, but it means you can only read your mail on one particular machine. Sometimes when you're away from home you might want to check your mail, so what do you do?

For this you need a *web mail* account. Here, the messages stay permanently on the mail server, and you read and reply to them using a regular web browser on any computer.

Does this mean you'll need two email addresses and you'll have to check for mail in two places? Possibly, though there's a lot of crossover these days. Yahoo! web mail accounts, for example, also have a regular POP server, so that you can view your mail online or have it downloaded automatically to your Mac. And most web mail services will also let you retrieve mail from your usual POP server so that you can get all your regular mail through a web browser – all you'll need is your username and password.

5.8 Organizing your mail

Setting up email accounts might sound technical, but if you take a methodical approach using the information provided by the email service, it's not hard. And, you only have to do it once.

Once that's done, you'll find the Mail application as easy to figure out as other Mac software. On the left is a Sidebar listing your *Inbox* (where all new messages arrive), *Reminders* (new to Leopard – see Section 12.3), and a list of any folders you've set up on your Mac to keep your mail organized. When you click on any of these items, a list of messages they contain appears in the main window to the right. Depending on how you've got the Mail display set up, you may also see a Preview window below this, so that when you click on a message, you can read its contents below. Otherwise, you just double-click on a message to view it in a new window.

The Mail Inbox is like the text message inbox on a mobile phone. However, where you might regularly delete text messages on your phone to save space, on the Mac there's no need to delete emails because they take up very little room compared with the size of the hard disk. Besides, you never know when you might need to refer to them much later. But while storage space isn't a problem, having an Inbox filling up with hundreds of messages most definitely is. Some messages can clearly be deleted (we'll look at *junk mail* and *spam* in a moment), but others need to be filed out of the way.

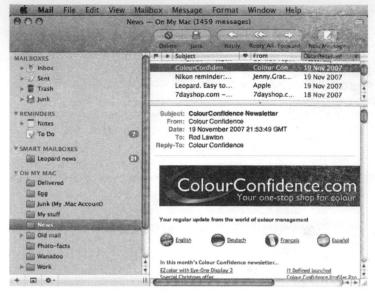

Mailboxes are folders for organizing and storing your messages, helping you to find them later. Here, we have a mailbox for News.

To do this, choose **New Mailbox** from the **Mailbox** menu (*Mailbox* is the name that Mail uses for an email folder). You can now drag messages out of the Inbox and into this new mailbox. Mailboxes can be organized just like folders in the Finder, so you can make your filing system as complicated (or as simple) as you like.

5.9 Sending and receiving mail

Sending an email is easy – just click the **New Message** button on the toolbar at the top of the window. You'll need to type in who the message is to, a title for the message and, finally, in the main window, the message itself.

Now you will need to know the other person's email address, obviously, and you can type this directly into the **To:** box. In practice, though, the sensible way of doing it is to add them to your Address Book instead – and you can open this by pressing the **Address Book** button on the toolbar.

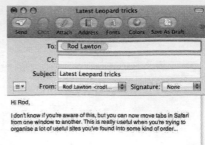

To send a message, click the Send button on the toolbar to show the message window. When you type a name into the To: box, Mail will automatically look it up in the Mac's Address Book.

Why is this smarter? Well, it's because you can now just type their name (or nickname) into the To: box of your message, and Mail will automatically look them up in the Address Book and insert their email address for you. It's a lot easer to type (and to remember) a person's name than it is their email address.

You don't need to do anything to receive emails – they arrive automatically because Mail checks for new messages at regular intervals. And if you want to reply to a message, you don't have to create a new message from scratch; instead, you can simply press the **Reply** button. Mail will automatically insert the other person's email address in your response.

There's a lot more to Mail than this, but you can explore it at your own pace using the online Help. There is one more thing you might like to know straight away, though – you can use Mail to send files to other people. You do this by typing the message and then pressing the **Attach** button on the message window's toolbar. This opens a dialog where you can locate the file you want to send on your hard disk.

One word of warning – don't send files bigger than 5Mb or so, because the other person's email server may reject the attachment for being too large.

5.10 Dealing with junk mail

While email has undoubtedly changed the way we communicate, it's also opened the floodgates to countless get-rich-quick schemes, advertisements, online scams and ghastly 'enhancement' products (and if you don't know what that means, consider yourself lucky). Mail calls this *Junk* and is pretty good at recognizing it automatically, and diverting it to the special *Junk* folder in the Sidebar. The process isn't perfect, though, and it's a good idea to click on this folder now and again to check its contents. If you find a message that actually isn't junk, press the **Not Junk** button on the toolbar. Similarly, if junk mail is still making it into your Inbox, click the offending message to select it and then press the **Junk** button to send it to the *Junk* folder.

Doing this helps to train Mail to recognize the junk you receive more reliably, so that after doing this for a few weeks you may find it's not making any more mistakes and that you don't need to check so often.

Summary

* Broadband routers enable you to connect several computers to the Internet via a single connection.

* Your broadband supplier will provide the information needed to configure your Mac or router.

* A wireless router will let you get online anywhere in the house.

* Your favourite web pages and their addresses can be stored as bookmarks in Safari.

* A search engine helps you find information online. The most popular is Google and it's built into the Safari toolbar.

* Buying online is straightforward and often more reliable than ordering by telephone because there's less scope for human error.

* You can download email messages to your Mac or view them online from any computer if you use a 'webmail' account.

* You can create Mailboxes (folders) to organize your email messages as they build up.

* Junk emails are a fact of life, but Mail can filter them out automatically.

06

iWork '08

In this chapter you will learn:

- what the iWork '08 programs do
- how to write a letter and design a leaflet in Pages
- how to create presentations and charts in Keynote
- the principles of spreadsheets
- how Numbers is different
- how to swap files with Microsoft Office users

6.1   What is iWork '08?

Macs are often thought of as creative or lifestyle computers, but they are actually very effective business tools too. Indeed, the world's best known office suite – Microsoft Office – is also available in a Mac version, and we'll be covering that in the next chapter. But Apple publishes its own, cheaper alternative to Microsoft Office. It's called iWork, and a 30-day trial version is included with new Macs.

Apple has recently launched iWork '08, which has seen many changes to the core programs Pages (word processing) and Keynote (presentations). The biggest change of all, though, is a new program called Numbers. Now iWork offers the same trio of applications you get in Microsoft Office – a word processor, a spreadsheet and a presentations tool. What's more, the applications in iWork are arguably more user-friendly and look more modern, and are certainly packed with neat touches to help you get your work done more quickly.

A 30-day trial version of iWork '08 is included with new Macs, but the full version is only £55 in the UK.

If you like what you see in the trial versions, you can purchase the full suite for just £55 (UK price), which makes iWork an amazing bargain in the light of what it can do.

6.2   Writing a letter in Pages

We'll start by taking a look at Pages, which is a word processing program with a difference, in that you can start with a blank page as usual or choose a ready-made design template.

These are not like the templates you get in Microsoft Word. A Pages template doesn't consist of just one page, but many different page layouts, so that you can choose a different layout for each page as you build up your document.

For now, though, we'll start with something simpler – writing a letter. In previous version of Pages, no distinction was made between ordinary word processor documents and more complicated page layouts. When you start Pages '08, though, you are presented with the *Template Chooser* which separates word processing templates from page layout templates.

There's a good reason for this. When you create an ordinary word processor document, you want it to keep adding pages automatically as you type. When you work on page layouts, though, you start with a fixed number of pages in mind and adjust the length or size of your text to suit. Other word processing programs (like Word, for example), don't offer this distinction and this can cause confusion where documents have to fit specific page lengths and with pages designed in a certain way.

Back to our letter...

1   You can start with a *Blank* template and create the letter from scratch, or choose one of the other letter templates. The *Typewriter* template looks good, so we'll use that.

2   You may find that the sheet in the typewriter image contains your name and contact details. Pages gets this from the user information you entered when you first set up your new Mac. To change any of this information, just double-click this object. You can now select any of the text by dragging the cursor over it, and type in new text instead.

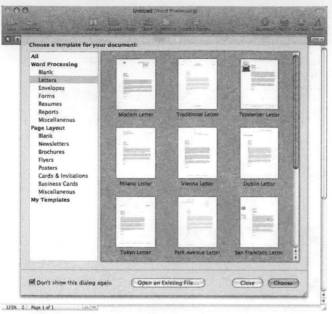

Choose a template.

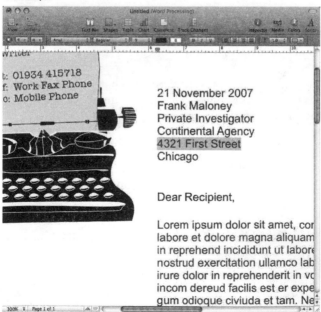

Check the contact details, and replace as needed.

3 Now you'll want to type in the name and address of the recipient. You'll find that simply clicking on a line selects the whole line. That's because this is *placeholder* text specifically designed for typing over, and it's widely used in Pages templates.

4 The main body of the letter is in what looks like Latin, but this is just dummy text. Again, clicking it once selects all this dummy text and you can simply type in the content of your own letter.

And that's it, you've used Pages to write a letter. You can now experiment with different fonts, sizes and styles for the text using the menus at the top of the window.

6.3 Designing a leaflet in Pages

Now let's try something a little more ambitious. Let's say you want to design a leaflet for your new business. If you take a look at the *Brochures* in the *Page Layout* section of the *Template Chooser*, you'll see there are quite a few to choose from. How about *Classic Brochure*?

1 The template opens up as a document that looks almost ready to print. All you have to do is type in your own text over the placeholder text that's in the template.

2 There may be other things you need to change, too, e.g. the photos in the template with some of your own. To do this, click the **Media** button at the top of the Pages window.

3 The **Media** palette has three sections, for *Audio*, *Photos* and *Music*. It's the Photos section that's relevant here, and if you select this you'll see that it displays the contents of your iPhoto library. How clever is that? It's typical of the way Apple seamlessly integrates all these different Mac applications.

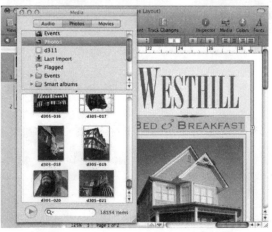

4 When you've found the photo you want in your library, drag it off the palette and onto the placeholder that you want to replace. Your new photo will be automatically sized to fit.

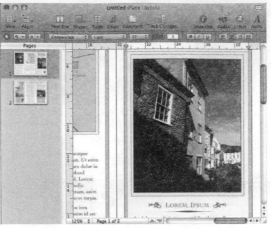

5 If you want to change the colours, click the **Inspector** button to display the **Inspector** palette. To change the colour of an object, click the palette's **Graphic** button, then click on the object. It's **Fill** colour will be displayed directly below, and to change the colour simply click on it and choose a new one from the Colors palette. To change the colour of text, double-click the box the text is in – this selects all the text. You can now click the Inspector's **Text** button to change the text colour.

In practice, some of the Pages templates are quite complex, with some objects layered on top of others, and it can take a little while to work out which items you need to edit and how, but the tools themselves are quite straightforward.

The most interesting feature, though, is to be found in the vertical *Pages* display at the far left of the screen. You'll see that templates often have two or more pages, and that these pages have different but themed layouts. You can add more pages at will, and you do this using the **Pages** button, top left.

And here's the next surprise – you can add ready-designed pages to those already in a document, and you have a choice of several layouts, depending on the template. You don't have to struggle to fill blank pages because they're already filled – all you have to do is type in your own text and add your own photos!

6.4 Creating a Keynote presentation

Word processing is one of the most common computing tasks of all, whether you're working in an office or writing a letter at home. But quite often we also need to produce presentations, and not just for work colleagues and customers – schools often ask students to submit homework and coursework as a presentation, too.

Presentations are effectively slideshows run from a computer and projected on to a screen in front of an audience. Usually, the author stands at the front talking through the main points, though this is not essential.

Microsoft Office users will be familiar with PowerPoint, its presentations tool. Apple's equivalent in iWork is Keynote.

If you've used PowerPoint, then you won't find it difficult to get to grips with Keynote. The principle is the same – the presentation is made up of a series of *slides* onto which you can place text and pictures. One slide can be made to fade into the next using *transitions*, and it's possible to make objects appear on the slides one by one as you explain your ideas to the audience.

Keynote, like Pages, comes with a collection of templates to make it easier to get started. These are themed presentation designs, and it has to be said that they are much more elegant and mod-ern-looking than those you get in Microsoft PowerPoint.

1 Once you've chosen the design, for example *Blueprint*, the first slide is created. In the case of the Blueprint theme, this is a title page with two text boxes which both say *Double-click to edit*. Do just that to enter your own title and strap line.

2 Now you're ready to start adding slides. To do this, click the '+' button in the top left-hand corner of the Keynote window.

This creates a new slide with a different layout that's still part of the overall design theme. If you don't like the layout or it's not suitable for the information you want to convey, click the **Masters** button at the top of the window and choose a new design.

3 To change the text, double-click a text box. To change a picture, open the **Media** palette and drag across a new one from your iPhoto library.

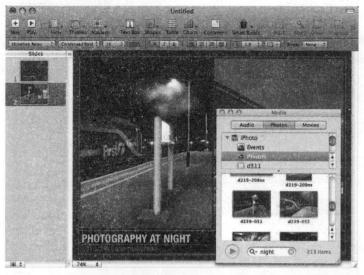

If you're unfamiliar with presentations, the best way to understand what Keynote can do is simply to experiment with slides and layouts and your own content, then play back the presentation to see what it looks like. To do this, select the first slide (they're displayed in the vertical *Slides* panel on the left) and click the **Play** button above.

6.5 Adding a chart

You can add more to Keynote slides than just words and pictures. You'll see that there are buttons at the top of the window for adding Shapes, Tables and Charts. These options are also available in Pages, by the way, and also in Numbers, which we'll come to shortly.

Explaining all of Keynote's features in depth would take up a whole book, whereas we only have a chapter in which to cover all three iWork programs. What we can do, though, is demonstrate just one of these features – charts.

Charts (or graphs) are a great way to present data in a more convincing or a more understandable fashion. Let's take a simple example. Imagine you're the treasurer of a club and that you need to illustrate how much is spent on premises, equipment and advertising as a proportion of the club's total outgoings.

1 Pie charts are ideal for illustrating this kind of data, so the first step is to create a new, blank slide and then click the **Charts** button to display a pop-up list of chart types – pie charts are near the bottom.

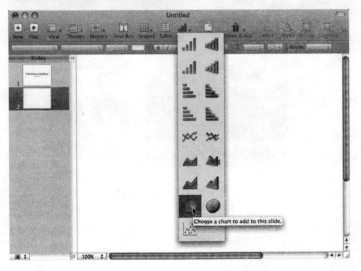

2 Keynote now creates a pie chart on the slide, together with a **Chart Data Editor** window which contains the data used to create the chart. Now at the moment, this contains dummy data you need to replace.

3 Double-click the cells in the **Data Editor** and type in your own data. Don't forget to change the row and column headings at the same time.

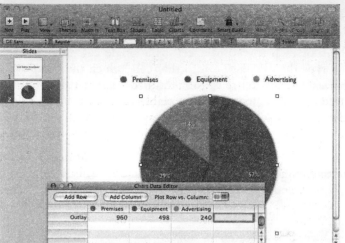

4 If there are extra columns of dummy data that you don't need, just click the column heading to select the whole column and press [**Backspace**] to delete it. To add columns or rows, just type directly into blank cells. When you make changes in the Data Editor window, the chart itself updates automatically.

6.6 Introducing spreadsheets

Finally, we'll take a look at Numbers, the brand new application in iWork '08. This is equivalent to the Excel spreadsheet program in Microsoft Office, though Numbers works slightly differently from Excel, so that even if you are already familiar with spreadsheet programs, you're going to find Numbers a little different, to say the least.

First things first, though. If you don't know anything about spreadsheets, they can seem extremely complex and daunting things. In principle, though, they are quite simple.

We all know how to work a pocket calculator. You enter a calculation, press the [=] key and the answer appears in the display. The trouble with calculators, though, is that they can only do one calculation at a time, and they forget the last one as soon as you begin the next.

A single spreadsheet is like a vast army of pocket calculators, all of which remember your calculations indefinitely.

Think of each spreadsheet cell as a single calculator's display. You type the calculation into that cell, which then displays the answer. The difference is, though, that these calculations can be based on the contents of other cells, and each cell has a unique reference (or 'address') to make this possible.

That's why spreadsheets use letters to identify columns and numbers for rows. Using a combination of column letter and cell number, you can identify each unique cell. This is called a *cell reference*, and it takes the form *A6*, or *G7* and so on.

A simple example will make this clearer.

1 Open a new Numbers document. You'll be presented with an empty spreadsheet.

2 Click on cell B2 and type in the number '2'. Click on cell B3 below it and type '2'. Now click on cell B4 below and type '=' and then click on cell B2. Now type a 'plus' sign ('+') and click on cell B3.

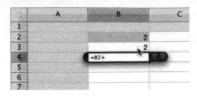

3 As you do this, you'll see that Numbers is recording your calculation in a black **Formula** box (formula is the spreadsheet term for a calculation). It should now read '=B2+B3'. If so, press the green tick button to the right.

4 Cell B4 now contains the result of adding cell B2 to cell B3. (We can now breathe a sigh of relief that 2 plus 2 does indeed equal 4.)

5 But now that we've set it up, this formula will continue to work even if we change the contents of cells B2 and B3. We can type in '16' and '23', for example, and it'll add these up too.

This is just scratching the surface, of course. Spreadsheets are capable of carrying out fiendishly complicated calculations in the blink of an eye, but this simple example should at least make it easier to understand how they do it.

6.7 What's different about Numbers

If you're used to conventional spreadsheet programs like Microsoft Excel, Numbers is going to look both familiar and strange at the same time. The spreadsheets themselves look much the same, but instead of extending off the screen as a practically infinite array of rows and columns, in Numbers they are a finite size. What you see on the screen is not the whole spreadsheet, but what Numbers calls a 'table'.

In fact, you can create many 'tables' on the same sheet, and they can be as big or as small as you like. This enables you to visually separate blocks of data, and this in turn makes it easier to understand and control how this data interacts.

Let's take a simple example. You want to prepare a list of your business's outgoings, and another listing sources of income. Then we can subtract one from the other to calculate the profit.

1 First, select the default table created in new documents by clicking its top left-hand corner and then press [**Backspace**] to delete it. This leaves you with a completely blank page.

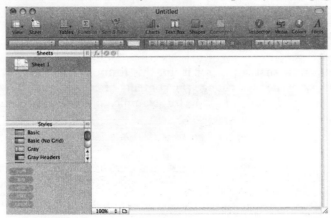

2 Now click the **Tables** button at the top of the window. This displays a list of table styles. We want the *Headers* table style.

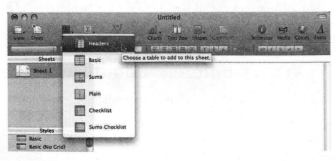

3 The new table has four columns for data where we only need one. To delete columns, move the mouse pointer over the right-hand side to display an arrow. Click this to open a drop-down menu and click the **Delete Column** option.

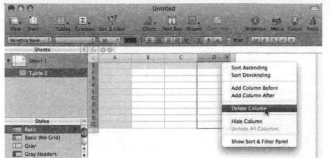

4 This leaves us with a table consisting of a single column with a title row and the top and row headings on the left. We can now type in our headings and data.

5 When that's done, we need to total up the individual outgoings. Select the empty cell directly below the column of figures, click the **Function** button at the top of the window and choose *Sum* from the menu. This cell will now display the total. If there are any blank rows left below, these can be deleted using the pop-up menus at the left-hand end of the rows.

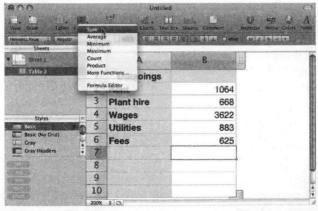

6 This process can be repeated for the company's sources of income. Finally, we can create a third, smaller table with just a heading ('Profit') and a single cell. To calculate the profit, we select this cell, type '=' and then click on the total income cell in the *Income* table. Next, we type '-' and then click on the total cell in the *Outgoings* table to complete the formula.

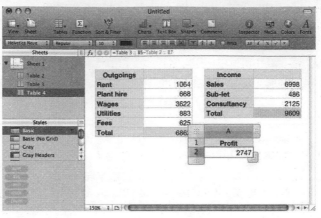

This hasn't achieved anything that couldn't have been done in Excel, but the data is now clearly separated and distinguished in different tables. The calculations are the same, but the way they're carried out is much easier to grasp visually.

This is not the only noteworthy characteristic of Numbers by any means. Charts too can be created as individual objects on the sheet, and you can add photos and other graphics to Numbers documents as readily as you can to Pages documents and Keynote slides. It's possible to create very sophisticated, compelling and graphically rich documents in Numbers and it's a much more sophisticated way of presenting data to clients and colleagues than a regular spreadsheet application like Excel can manage.

6.8   Swapping documents with others

Of course, not everyone you work with will be using iWork. You may frequently find yourself swapping files with Microsoft Office users (PC or Mac), so you may be faced with the problem of opening Office files that others send you or finding ways to send them files created in iWork that they can open using their Microsoft Office applications.

The best way to do this is to find a file format that both sets of programs can work with. Now iWork can open Office 2003 (PC) and Office 2004 (Mac) files directly, whether they were created in Word, Excel or PowerPoint. Office 2007 on the PC is a slightly different case because Microsoft has introduced a brand new file format, but iWork '08 can read these files directly too.

Transferring files the other way, from iWork to Office, may not be so straightforward. The problem is that the iWork applications offer some features which simply don't exist in their Office counterparts, and this is especially true of Numbers.

The iWork applications can, however, export documents in Office formats and attempt to preserve the document formatting and features as far as possible in the process.

Ultimately, though, if a large part of your work does involve swapping files with Office users, you might be better off using Office yourself. Paradoxically, this is not because iWork is inferior. In fact, it's because there are things you can do in iWork which simply don't have counterparts in Office. Sometimes you just have to accept the lowest common denominator...

Summary

* iWork is Apple's alternative to Microsoft Office.

* Pages can produce either regular text documents or sophisticated page layouts.

* Keynote can be used to produce presentations for meetings or training sessions.

* Numbers is a very new and different kind of spreadsheet program.

* iWork '08 can open Microsoft Office files directly.

* To send iWork files to Microsoft Office users it's necessary to choose a file format that Office programs can open.

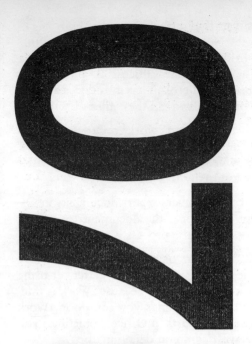

7 Mac Office 2004

In this chapter you will learn:

- why Office makes sense for Mac users
- how the Mac and Windows versions of Office compare
- how to get started with Word
- about outlines in Word
- how to add graphics to documents
- about Excel's List Manager
- how to create a PowerPoint presentation
- what Entourage can do

7.1 No Mac is an island!

There was a time when using a Mac meant that you risked cutting yourself off from the regular world of PCs, and swapping files or any kind of data could be a difficult, technical process. That was long ago. Today, Macs and PCs co-exist perfectly happily, and this is explained in much more detail in Chapter 8.

This co-existence is easier still if the PC and Mac users are using the same software, because files can then be opened, viewed and edited on both machines without any kind of conversion. Your PC-using colleague can send you an Excel worksheet to amend, you can modify it on your Mac, send it back and they can open it again just as if it had been worked on using a PC.

That's the big advantage of using Microsoft Office on a Mac for those in a business environment populated largely by Windows PCs (and such environments tend to use Microsoft Office applications almost exclusively).

Office on the Mac is almost identical to the PC version, with Word, Excel and PowerPoint, but it has its own personal information manager, Entourage.

Microsoft Word

Microsoft Excel

Microsoft PowerPoint

Microsoft Entourage

7.2 Mac Office vs Windows Office

The Mac and Windows versions share the same core applications: Word, Excel and PowerPoint, but there are differences in the secondary applications.

The main difference is that the Windows version of office comes with an email/personal organizer application called Outlook, which doesn't have a Mac version. Instead, Mac users get a program called Entourage. This does the same job, managing your mail, your contacts, appointments and tasks, but looks and works very differently.

The Windows version of Office comes in several editions, too, and the higher-level editions include programs not available on the Mac, notably the Access relational database application (too technical for everyday users) and the Publisher desktop publishing application (Pages can do this job very well on the Mac).

There are minor differences too between the Mac and PC versions of Word, PowerPoint and Excel, but these are mostly down to the look and feel of the interface. The Mac versions use a floating Formatting Palette while the PC versions rely on toolbars or ribbons, depending on the version (Office 2003 or 2007).

For those who mainly use Word, Excel and PowerPoint, there's really not much to choose between the Mac and PC versions at all, and Mac Office 2004 is in no way the poor relation to Windows Office 2003 or 2007.

7.3 Mac Office vs iWork '08

By now, you may have spotted that the three core applications in Mac Office – word processor, spreadsheet and presentations tool – are matched by the same three program types in Apple's iWork '08. So should you use Office, or should you use iWork?

iWork is much cheaper, different, but equally powerful in its own way and, it has to be said, it looks and behaves like it belongs to a new generation of software, whereas Office 2004 is definitely 'old school'. For domestic users who don't have to swap files with Windows machines on a regular basis, iWork is more attractive and simpler. But for those who work alongside PCs all day, whether on the same site or via email, Office 2004 is the most practical solution because there are no difficulties over inconsistencies in the way documents are formatted. This becomes particularly important if you have to collaborate with others over documents, financial worksheets or presentations.

7.4 Microsoft Word basics

When you launch Microsoft Word, it doesn't create a new, blank document straight away. Instead, it launches into the Project Gallery, where Office 2004's collection of templates for Word, Excel and PowerPoint are combined into a single window. You may find this useful if you regularly use the templates supplied with the program, but you may find it annoying if you prefer to start from scratch or from existing documents (it also appears when you start Excel or PowerPoint).

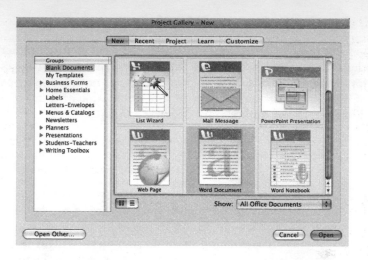

When you start Word, Excel or PowerPoint you can choose a ready-made document template from the Project Gallery.

To disable it, click the Gallery's last section, **Customize**, and de-select the box labelled **Show Project Gallery at startup**.

To create a new, blank Word document, either select this option in the Project Gallery's **New** section or, if you have disabled the Project Gallery as we've just described, Word will simply start up with a new, blank document.

Try it out – just start typing. To change the font, text size or style, just select the text by dragging the cursor over it and choose the options you want to change from the toolbar running across the top of the screen.

But you can also make adjustments using the Formatting palette. If it's not visible, use the **View > Formatting Palette** menu command. This palette is arranged vertically in a series of sections, each of which can be expanded by clicking the arrow to the left of its title and collapsed by clicking the arrow again.

You can use the Formatting Palette to add objects like tables and graphics, format text and apply predefined text styles. These styles include a series of headings, labelled 'Heading 1', 'Heading 2' and so on. These have a special significance in Word, as we'll see in the next section.

7.5 Outlining in Word

In some respects, Word looks distinctly old-fashioned and rather clunky, compared with Pages. Nevertheless, it has advantages for technical and academic authors which are outside the scope of this book, and another specific advantage which will make a difference to any author – it's called *Outlining*.

Outlining isn't so much a software tool as a way of working, and while other word processors have supported outlining to a degree, it's only in Microsoft Word that it's done (in the author's opinion) properly.

Word has a special Outline mode. You can enter it by choosing **Outline** from the **View** menu. Once you're in this mode you're able to organize, develop and structure your ideas in a way that's simply not possible with conventional, 'linear' writing. Here's a quick introduction to how it works:

1 First, you'll note that in Outline mode, each paragraph has a square symbol to its left. This is used for dragging paragraphs from one place to another or for selecting the whole paragraph with a single click. The significance of this will become apparent shortly.

2 Imagine you're writing an essay. The subject doesn't matter – it can be anything you like. Don't even try to organize it into a logical order in your head before you start typing. Instead, type in every idea on a single line, as it occurs to you. Keep going until you've written down everything you can think of for the time being. You should now have a long list of ideas. This is the raw material; the starting point. It's similar to a technique called *free writing* which is used by some authors.

It's much more important to first get everything down – you can sort it out into some kind of order later. And that's the next step in the Outlining process.

3 Go back over your list. You'll notice two things. The first is that many of the ideas are in the wrong order. This is easy to put right. To move an item, simply drag its square symbol up or down, reorganizing your ideas into something like their correct order.

4 But you'll also notice something else. Not all of your ideas will be of equal significance. Some will be sub-topics of others – and this is where you can start organizing them into a hierarchy of headings and subheadings. Start by picking a main topic – click on the square symbol to its left to select it. Now use the **[Shift]-[Tab]** shortcut. This *promotes* the topic to a heading.

5 Find any subheadings for this topic. Make sure they're moved up so that they're beneath the heading, select one of these topics and hit **[Tab]**. This demotes the topic to a subheading. (To start with, all the topics are in the body text style. This is the lowest of the low in the heading hierarchy.)

6 Now you can go through all the topics, moving them, promoting them and demoting them until they're organized into a hierarchical structure.

7 As you do this, you'll start to see other topics that need adding, and spot connections to other areas that you should include and explore. The outlining process encourages your mind to think 'outwards', where conventional writing tends to focus it 'inwards' along very linear paths. When you're satisfied that your outline is complete, your document will consist of a complete set of headings and subheadings.

- Photography
- History
- Practitioners
- Cameras
- Film
- Digital
- Black and white
- Colour
- Art
- Commercial
- Newspapers
- Lenses
- Shutter speed
- Privacy
- Prints

Photography
- History
- Practitioners
- Cameras
- Lenses
- Film
- Digital
- Black and white
- Colour

Photography
- *History*
- *Practitioners*
- *Cameras*
  - Lenses
  - Film
  - Digital
  - Black and white
  - Colour
  - Art

Photography
- *History*
- *Practitioners*
- *Equipment*
  - Cameras
  - Lenses
- *Technique*
  - Shutter speed
  - Cataloguing
  - Editing

8 With this structure in place, writing the main body text is suddenly so much easier because now you know what you've got to write! To use the body text style, use the [**Shift**]-[**Command**]-[**N**] shortcut, or choose **Normal** from the text style menu on the toolbar. This outlining system completely banishes the dreaded 'blank page' syndrome that can stop even experienced writers dead in their tracks.

⋄ **Photography**
  ▫ *History*
  ▫ *Practitioners*
  ⋄ *Equipment*
    ▫ Cameras
    ▫ Lenses
  ⋄ *Technique*
    ▫ Shutter speed
    ▫ Cataloguing
    ▫ Editing
  ⋄ *Sharing pictures*
    ▫ Prints
    ▫ Slideshows
    ▫ Albums
    ▫ Online
  ⋄ *The recording medium*
    ⋄ Film
      ▫ Over the past ten years digital imaging technology has advanced at breakneck pace. At the beginning of this period, digital cameras were expensive and produced very poor picture quality compared to film. By its end, digital cameras have more or less replaced film completely, at least for amateur photographers and enthusiasts.
    ▫ Digital
    ▫ Black and white
    ▫ Colour

When you've filled in the body text, you can revert to **Normal** or **Page Layout** view using the **View** menu. Page Layout view is best if you want to see exactly how your pages will print as you work, and especially if you want to insert graphics or photos.

7.6 Inserting graphics in Word

It's easy to add graphics to a Word document either by dragging them from a Finder window on to the document window, or by opening the **Insert** menu and choosing the **Picture** command.

If you drag graphics on to the document, you'll see the insertion point moving around the text as you drag the mouse pointer. This indicates where the graphic will be inserted when you release the mouse button. If you use the menu command instead, first place the insertion point where you want the graphic to go.

By default, Word inserts graphics as *inline* objects. That means they are embedded in the text, so that if the text moves because of editing changes, the graphic moves with it. This can be useful, but sometimes you want the graphic to stay where you put it and for the text to flow around it, as it might on a magazine page. To do this, change the graphic's *text wrap* properties.

1 Click on the graphic to select it, and expand the **Wrapping** section in the **Formatting** palette (you need to be in Normal or Page Layout view to do this, not Outline view).

2 Click on the **Style** button to display a list of wrap options. The current setting is **In Line With Text**, but if you change it to **Square**, for example, the text will now flow around the graphic, which will stay where it is even if the text moves.

Actually, that's not quite true. The graphic is still *anchored* to the text to the extent that it will move to another page if the text it's anchored to does. This is Microsoft's attempt to make Word foolproof, but in fact it makes it terribly confusing for those attempting to use Word like a desktop publishing program, when its behaviour can seem utterly unpredictable.

If you are interested in producing sophisticated page layouts, you are in fact much better off with Pages.

Pinhole photography

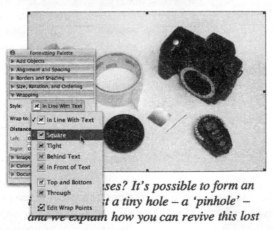

...ses? It's possible to form an ... t a tiny hole – a 'pinhole' – and we explain how you can revive this lost

It's easy to insert pictures in Word documents, but you do need to understand how the text wrapping options work.

7.7 Excel basics

Microsoft Excel has long been considered the standard professional spreadsheet application amongst statisticians, engineers, accountants and many other technical professionals.

We have explained in Chapter 6 how spreadsheets work. What we will do here is highlight an area in Excel which is often overlooked – its ability to create and manage *lists*. And the Mac version of Excel does this far more effectively than Office 2004 for Windows.

List is another word for database. You could, for example, prepare a list of invoices to customers. Here's how it's done:

1 First, use the **Insert > List** menu command. This runs the List wizard, which walks you through the process in three steps. First, you're asked where your list data is (this only applies if you already have data which you want to convert into a list) and where you want the list to be created – select **New worksheet**.

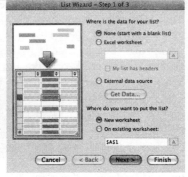

2 Now click the **Next** button to go to step 2. Here you're asked to choose the column headings for your list. In our example, we want the first column to have the heading 'Job', so we type 'Job' into the **Column name** box and click the **Add** button.

3 We need to add a column for the customer name, so now we type 'Customer' into the box and click the **Add** button again.

4 Next, we need a column heading for 'Amount', but here the procedure is slightly different. Before clicking **Add,** open the **Data type** pop-up menu directly below the box and choose **Currency** from the list.

5 Add a fourth column heading, 'Date due', and this time choose **Date** from the **Data type** menu.

6 Click the **Next** button. We're now on step 3, where we can choose a name for the list (if required) and check the **Show totals row** box. Now click **Finish.**

The finished list doesn't look like a regular worksheet. The usual spreadsheet grid is gone, and the list is isolated in its own white space. The headings are separated from the first row, which is empty. Start by typing in the first invoice. As you do, you'll notice that Excel creates a new, blank line directly below. This is ready for you to type in the next invoice, and so on. You'll also see a 'Total row' appear at the bottom.

Type in some more invoices. By default, the Total row totals up the last column. This is the due date for our invoices, so the total is meaningless. To fix this, click the pop-up in the right-hand corner of that Total cell and choose (**No formula**) from the list. Now, click the pop-up in the Total cell under the 'Amount' column, and choose **Sum** from the list. Now, this cell will display the total value of all our invoices. This assumes special significance when we look at the AutoFilters for each column...

The column headings each have a pop-up menu alongside them, too. These are the *AutoFilters*. You can use these menus to do two things: (a) to sort your invoices by Job, Customer and so on, depending on which column heading you're working with, and (b) to 'filter' the data according to a specific Job, Customer and so on. These menus list each unique name or value in that column, so identifying and selecting them is easy.

When you AutoFilter a column in this way, two things happen. The first is that the list now only shows those matching items. Second, the Total row now adds up only the items currently being shown. For example, you could do this to isolate all the jobs you've done for a particular customer and get a total amount owed by that customer for those jobs.

Excel's Lists offer a very quick and useful way of compiling and analysing information. And they remain quick (and become even more useful!) when you have hundreds or even thousands of records to sort through.

Excel's Lists are self-contained databases which you can filter and sort using the menus at the top of the columns. You can also add a Total Row.

7.8 PowerPoint basics

PowerPoint is Microsoft Office's presentations tool. Many computer users might go through their whole career without ever needing to create a presentation, or even knowing what one is, but increasingly they're becoming part of the armoury of any keen executive. They're also creeping into schools as students are encouraged more and more to use PowerPoint to develop their essays, coursework and class presentations.

PowerPoint can look complicated, but presentations are actually quite simple. Once you understand the principles they're based on, everything falls into place. In addition, PowerPoint is really very similar to Apple's Keynote, described in Chapter 6. Once you understand one, you understand the other.

Every presentation is basically a slideshow. And each *slide* is a single screen of information. This information could be a title, a heading, a series of bullet points, a chart, a photo or a diagram – or combinations of all of those.

When you make your presentation you show each slide in turn, pausing as necessary to explain certain points in more depth. To make your presentations look more professional, you can add *transitions* to make one slide fade into the next, and you can *animate* objects on the slide so that bullet points appear one by one, for example.

Using PowerPoint can be as simple or as complicated as you want to make it. It's best to start with something simple, like one of the preset templates, and experiment with the more advanced options as you go along.

Let's imagine you need to present a new product to the sales team at your company...

1   First, start up PowerPoint to display the **Project Gallery** and look down the list of projects on the left to find **Presentations**. Clicking the arrow to the right of this will expand the list to show two sub-categories – **Content** and **Design**.

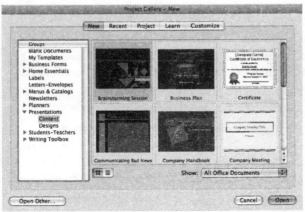

2   Design templates are for when you know what you need to say, but you're looking for a ready-made presentation design which will complement your message. But if you're new to presentations, you'll need a little help simply planning what needs to go into the presentation, so click **Content** instead.

This displays a selection of designs in the main window to the right. Each one is labelled with the style of presentation – the *Products and Services* template looks just what we need, and we can double-click it to open it.

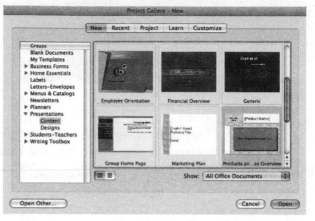

3 PowerPoint will start, and the template should be displayed in Normal view. Down the left-hand side of the window is an outline of the contents. Each main heading corresponds to a slide in the presentation, and subheadings underneath are sub-headings on the slide. (Outlines in PowerPoint are really just like the outlines in Word, which we looked at earlier in this chapter.) To the right, in the main part of the window, is the currently-selected slide. Clicking on a different heading in the outline on the left will display a different slide.

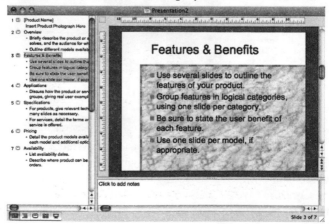

4 The presentation's already been set up to list the main points you'll need to make in a presentation of this type, so it's simply a case of typing your own words over those currently on the slides – these are usually reminders of what you've got to do or examples of things you should write. To replace this text, click on the box it's in and then drag over it as you would in a word processor to select it and then type your own words.

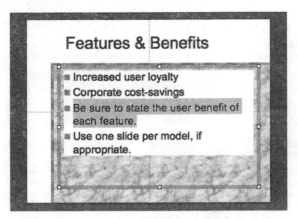

5 Now go through the whole presentation doing this, typing your own titles, explanations and bullet points – you'll have a finished presentation in no time. You might also want to experiment with adding photos or diagrams where available. To do this, open the **Insert** menu and choose **Picture**.

6 Finally, you may decide that the style and colours of the presentation aren't really to your liking. The great thing about PowerPoint is that both of these can be changed at any time across the whole presentation. First, if the **Formatting** palette isn't visible, display it using the **View** menu. Now expand the last section called **Change Slides** and select the first of the three tabs, labelled **Slide Design**.

7 You'll see that this contains thumbnail images of a whole range of different slide designs. When you click on one, all the slides in the presentation are updated with that design.

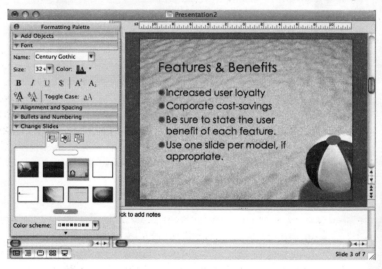

Obviously there's a lot more to PowerPoint than this, but the key to getting up and running quickly with this program, as with so many others, is to start with something simple that makes sense straight away, and then build on that as and when you're ready to take on more complicated ideas.

7.9 Entourage – unique to the Mac

While the Mac's versions of Word, Excel and PowerPoint are quite similar to the Windows version, there's no Mac version of Outlook, the email and personal information manager on the PC. Instead, Microsoft developed a wholly new application called Entourage, which does the same jobs, but looks very different from Outlook. Entourage is a single program, but with six distinct sections: Mail, Address Book, Calendar, Notes, Tasks and Project Centre. These are accessed by buttons clustered in the top left-hand corner of the Entourage window.

If you click the **Mail** button, you'll see a list of mail folders on the left, and a list of messages in the current folder on the right – though the layout can be customized, so yours may be different. For example, you can use the **View > Preview Pane** command to display a preview pane either below the messages or to its right. When you click on a message title, its contents are displayed in this pane. Entourage's online Help explains the display and other options available, so we won't go into detail here. (The basics of email are explained in Chapter 5.) The one other thing you will need to know is how to set up your email accounts in Entourage. For this, use the **Tools > Accounts** command to open the **Accounts** window, and click the **New** button to create an account. The **Account Setup Assistant** then walks you through the process in easy steps – you will need the email account information from your service provider or email host.

But why would you want to use Entourage for email when you already have the Mail program supplied with the Mac? It's largely a matter of preference. Your author prefers Mail, but others may prefer Entourage – it is sometimes useful to be able to link emails with appointments and appointments with files. This integration of your office tasks is what Entourage is designed for.

The Address Book is where Entourage stores email addresses, phone numbers and street addresses. Your lists of contacts can be sorted alphabetically by name or company, for example, by clicking the column headings at the top of the lists. Again, the Mac already has an Address Book of its own, so whether or not you'll find the Entourage Address Book useful will depend on how you like to work and how useful you find Entourage to be.

It's the same situation with the Calendar. Here, you can plan holidays, enter appointments and set up meetings – when you set up a meeting, you can also invite people in your Address Book by email with just a few button clicks. You may find this kind of integration of your office tasks indispensable, but be aware that it can also force you into an unnecessarily complex and regimented way of working – it's a double-edged sword. The Calendar in Entourage is an alternative to Apple's own iCal. Again, the decision you face is whether to use the Apple software that comes with the Mac for these jobs, or whether to move all your data across into Entourage. They don't share the same data, so it's going to have to be one or the other.

The Notes section is a place where you can jot down ideas or information that don't justify an entire document on their own, while the Tasks section is where you list all the jobs you've got to do, the date they have to be done by and their priority. The Apple alternative to this is the To Do list in iCal and Mail.

It's clear, then, that Entourage is a very sophisticated personal organizer application that can do a great job of keeping your work life running smoothly. It's also clear, though, that you can do pretty well all of these things using the free Apple software pre-installed on the Mac.

Entourage has six sections, accessed by the buttons top left: Mail, Address Book, Calendar, Notes, Tasks, Project Center.

So which do you use? On the one hand, Entourage integrates all these jobs very well and also dovetails very well with the other Office 2004 applications. However, other programs apart from Office are more likely to integrate with the Apple software. You may also find the Apple alternatives rather simpler to understand and more direct in their approach.

7.10 Managing your projects

But for managers with a very organized approach to their work, Entourage has the advantage. And this is reflected in its sixth section, the Project Center. Here's how it works:

1 Click the **New Project** button and type in a title. Let's call it 'Teach Yourself Basic Mac Skills'. We also need to set a deadline (November 14th – private joke – ahem) and, if we have a suitable image, we can drag it into the box on the right as a visual reminder. Underneath, you can jot down any relevant notes about the project, if applicable.

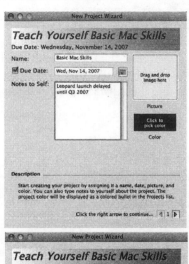

2 In the next step, you can create or set up *Project Watch* folders. Any documents or other items added to these folders subsequently will automatically appear in that project in Entourage.

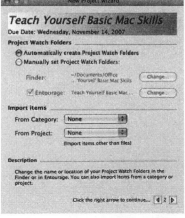

3 In the next step you can instruct Entourage to automatically associate emails from Project contacts with the project (more on this shortly), or emails about specific subjects.

4 The fourth step is a summary of your settings, and when you OK this step, you're returned to the Project Center where you can view your new project. This has a number of dif-

ferent tabs, but the first is the *Overview*. This displays a calendar at the top, a task window below and, at the bottom a list of related email messages and documents. As time goes by, these lists will be populated automatically.

5 Finally, you will need to associate relevant contacts with the project, and you do this using the **Contacts** tab and clicking the **Add** button to select them from your Address Book.

There's a lot more to Entourage's Project Center than we have the space to cover here, but this simple walkthrough should have made it easier to see what it sets out to do and how it works. It's when you undertake complex management tasks like these that Entourage begins to pull its weight, but we repeat our earlier warning that Entourage can lure you into setting up procedures which appear efficient but are actually rather more complex and bureaucratic than they need to be.

7.11 Office 2008 is coming

These descriptions of the tools, functions and uses of the Office applications relate to Office 2004. A major new version, Office 2008, is just around the corner. This was due in the latter part of 2007, but its launch was delayed, which is why this chapter is devoted to the older version on sale at the time of going to press.

Office 2008 looks set to be a major upgrade, and it's not just a reworked interface. The main thrust seems to be towards faster, easier document creation, and graphically richer documents. Drag and drop *Elements* will make it easier to add objects to your documents, *Smart Art* should help you get your data across in more meaningful and compelling ways, and Entourage's *My Day* window lets you see how your day is shaping up while you're working in other applications. Word's new *Publishing Layout* looks especially interesting, offering the kind of simple and intuitive page layout that's previously only been available in Pages.

It should be worth waiting for!

Summary

+ Microsoft Office on the Mac is largely the same as Office on the PC. It's ideal for those who need to swap files with PC-based colleagues.

+ Word's outlining mode is a unique tool for organizing ideas.

+ You can import graphics into Word documents, but it's not the ideal program for fancy page layouts.

+ Excel isn't just a spreadsheet program – it's great as a database too, thanks to its list tools.

+ PowerPoint's presentations may look dull, but it's good at getting you started.

+ Entourage is the Mac equivalent of Outlook on the PC. It is good for project management, but can draw you into over-complex routines.

+ Entourage competes with Apple's Address Book, iCal and Mail programs, and these are more widely supported.

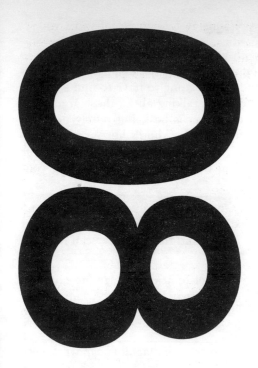

08

working with PCs

In this chapter you will learn:

- how to transfer files by email
- ways to transfer larger files via the Internet
- the relative usefulness of CDs, DVDs, hard disks and stick drives
- how to connect to a PC network
- how to make sure files are compatible

8.1   Swapping files

You may be delighted with your new Mac, but you still have to get on with other computer users. The vast majority of computers out there are PCs, and you're going to have to find a way to work alongside them. We're not talking about those arguments in the pub about which computer is best, but purely practical considerations, like transferring your child's homework assignment to the PCs at school, or working on your boss's report when he or she uses a PC at the office and you're using your Mac at home.

There are two issues here. One is finding a way to get files from the Mac to the PC and vice versa. The other is making sure that the PC can read the Mac's files, and that the Mac can read the PC's.

Windows PCs make little attempt to acknowledge the existence of Macs or work with them. Fortunately, Apple, recognizing the Mac's minority status perhaps, have gone to great lengths to accommodate Windows PCs.

We'll look at ways of making sure both machines can work with the same files, but first we'll look at how to get these files from one computer to the other. A few years ago this might have been a bit of a stumbling block, but now it's easy.

Send files by email or the Internet

Just about everyone, whether they own an PC or a Mac, uses email. And as long as the files aren't too large (anything under 5Mb should be fine) you can simply attach the file to the email. It's as simple as that. You have to make sure the file is one that the PC can read, of course, and we'll look at that a little later in this chapter. Other than that, sending files between Macs and PCs via email is no different from sending them from one PC to another the same way.

But what do you do about files too large to email? You can use a go-between site like www.yousendit.com. It's a really clever system – you upload your file to the YouSendIt site, and at the same time an email is sent to the recipient telling them where to go to download it. Files remain available for a few days – long enough for the other person to fetch them at their leisure. This service is free for light personal use (businesses have to pay) and it has a huge 100Mb file limit. It's unlikely you'll ever need to send anything larger than this and, if you do, use one of the following methods.

As long as the file's no larger than around 5Mb, the easiest way to send it to someone else is as an email attachment.

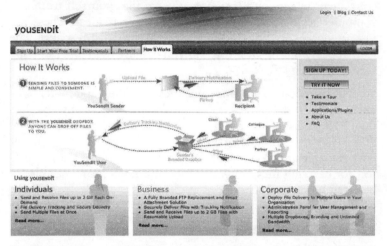

You can send files up to 100Mb in size via the Internet using the free transfer service at www.yousendit.com

Burn a CD

When you insert a blank CD into your Mac's CD-ROM drive, its icon appears on the desktop and you can copy files to it as you would any other drive – up to the CD's maximum 650–700Mb limit.

When you've copied the files across, you then *burn* the CD, a process which takes a few minutes. Once that's done, you can eject the CD and send it to the other person. CDs are cheap, so while it might be inconvenient for it to be lost or damaged in transit, it's hardly going to break the bank. And given the low cost, you don't need to worry about getting the other person to send it back, either.

Use a stick drive

CDs are cheap and disposable, but you can only use them once and they're comparatively slow for saving and accessing data. They also have a limited capacity. You could use a DVD instead, but these are also a little slow and inconvenient to prepare, too. CDs and DVDs are good for sending data away, they're less convenient when you just want to carry files yourself from one computer to another. For this a stick drive is ideal. These are just an inch or so long and plug straight into a USB socket. The icon appears on the Desktop and you can use the Finder to copy files and folders across.

Stick drives come in various capacities, and they're now remarkably cheap. In the UK, a 1Gb stick drive will typically cost less than £10, and you can get them in capacities up to 4Gb or even 8Gb. They offer much higher capacities than CDs, much faster data transfer and they can be re-used indefinitely. They're perfect for carrying files between office and home, for example, or between home and school.

External hard disks

The next step up is a portable external hard disk. These too plug into a USB socket, and this is where they get their power – there's no need for a separate power cable. This makes them very convenient for carrying around in a briefcase, say.

External hard disks come in varying capacities, starting at around 80Gb and going all the way up to 250Gb. They're perfect for transferring files between Macs and PCs (though they do have to be formatted for a PC, not a Mac) and they're also useful for keeping backups of your important files.

Nowadays, then, it's just as easy to swap files between Macs and PCs as it is between one PC and another.

8.2 Joining a network

There is another way to swap files between a Mac and a PC and that's by connecting them on a network. You can set up a small network from scratch to link a PC and a Mac, or you can connect the Mac to an existing PC network. Corporate networks in large offices are complex things and you'd need to check with the network administrator to find out what you'd need to do. In the home, though, it's much simpler. A home or small office network will consist of two or more machines connected to a router. The router handles all the data traffic between these computers. (We met routers in Chapter 5.)

When a Mac (or a PC) is on a network, it can see the other machines on the network, but can only access those folders which the users of those machines have specifically set up for sharing. It's the same on the Mac – the other computers on the network can only see your shared folders, not the entire contents of your hard disk.

The Mac's online Help system explains the basics of networking in more detail than we have the space for here. The important thing to understand is that connecting to a PC network isn't just possible, it's easy.

On machines running Tiger, you needed to click the **Network** icon in the Finder Sidebar and then browse the network for the computer or computers you wanted to connect to. That wasn't difficult, but Leopard has made it easier still. The Finder Sidebar now has a *Shared* section which lists any other computers on the network. You can click on any of these machines to see what shared folders exist on each, and then click on these folders to access the contents.

It's good practice to set up user names and passwords for shared folders. If these are required for any of the computers you access over the network, you'll be asked to type them into a dialog.

8.3 Common file types

There are many ways to transfer files between Macs and PCs, but you also need to make sure that each machine can make sense of the other's files. This used to be quite a problem, and there were all sorts of third-party file-conversion programs on the market. Now, thankfully, none of this is necessary any more.

The fact is that many files are of a standard type that can be read by both machines. For example, digital photos are usually in the JPEG file format, or sometimes the TIFF format or the RAW format used by some professional cameras. These files are all freely interchangeable between Macs and PCs. So are music files in the MP3 format. iTunes uses its own format, admittedly, but can be configured to record CD tracks as MP3s.

Sometimes people compress files which are to be sent as email attachments. This is almost always done using the *Zip* compressed file format on the PC, and now the Mac supports Zip files directly too.

The Mac now uses the same .zip compressed file format as Windows PCs. You can create zip archives directly in the Finder.

Ch07-office.zip

And even if you're using Pages, Keynote and Numbers on the Mac where your work colleagues are using Microsoft Word, PowerPoint and Excel, it's not a problem because the Mac's iWork applications can open these file types directly. When you save your work, choose a format that Microsoft Office can read – like the Word *doc* format, for example, when saving a Pages document, while in Numbers you should export spreadsheets in the Excel format.

Where the same software is being used on both computers, there isn't a problem. Microsoft Office users can swap files from Mac to PC and back again without a hitch (although we may have to wait until Office 2008 on the Mac to get full compatibility with the new file formats in Office 2007 on the PC). It's the same when you're working with photo-montages in Adobe Photoshop or professional page layouts in InDesign.

Where the applications are different, you simply need to find a common file format that both applications understand. This happens when you're swapping files between PCs, too, if they don't both have the same software. It's difficult to generalize about this because each set of circumstances is different, but there's almost always a way of finding a format for transferring

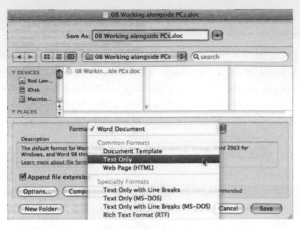

If you and the other person are using different programs, you'll need to save your files in a format the other person can read.

data between two different programs. For example, database programs all use their own specific file formats, but you can use a simple comma separated values (CSV) file format that both programs understand to swap data between them. Where there's a will there's a way!

For the most part, transferring files between Macs and PCs is no more difficult than transferring them between one Mac and another or one PC and another. There is, however, one technical difference between Macs and PCs you should be aware of...

File types and extensions

With both Macs and PCs you can simply double-click a file to open it. The computer knows which program to launch to do this because that information is embedded in the file. But it's done in different ways.

Windows users will know that files have three-letter *extensions* which identify the file type, such as '.jpg' for JPEG files or '.doc' for Microsoft Word documents. These extensions may be hidden, depending on the view options chosen in Windows Explorer, but they're still there and they're vital because Windows needs them to identify the file type and hence the program needed to open them.

Macs don't need file extensions. The creator information is embedded invisibly in the file data.

If you get a file from a PC it will have a three-letter extension on the end, but the Mac tolerates this perfectly well. What can happen, though, is that if you create a file on the Mac and omit the three-letter extension on the end, when you send it to a PC owner they can't open it. Without the extension, the PC won't know what sort of file it is and what to do with it.

One solution is to add the extension manually in Windows. The other is to make sure you always add extensions to filenames on the Mac. It's good practice, because you never know when these files might be needed on a PC.

Don't worry, though – you don't have to memorize dozens of file type extensions and type them in manually. Most Mac applications will add them automatically when you save the file – if not, there's usually an option you can select which activates this.

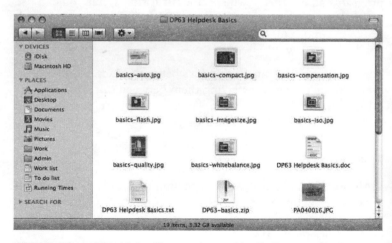

Windows PCs use three-letter file extensions to identify file types. The Mac doesn't need these but displays them anyway to remain compatible with PCs.

Summary

+ It's often easiest to transfer files via email or the Internet.

+ CDs are inexpensive, but comparatively cumbersome for transferring files.

+ Portable hard disks and stick drives are quick and convenient, and can be re-used indefinitely.

+ Macs can connect to PC networks easily.

+ Macs and PCs can often work with the same files without conversion.

+ Where different programs are involved, it's always possible to find a common file format which both can work with.

09

iPhoto

In this chapter you will learn:

- how iPhoto organizes your photos
- how to import photos from a camera
- how to view your photos
- how to organize photos with Albums
- how to find photos with keywords and Smart Albums
- how to add ratings and comments to photos
- how to share photos with others

9.1   What is iPhoto?

iPhoto is supplied pre-installed with all new Macs. It's a photo cataloguing program which can also edit and enhance pictures, print them out and create greetings cards, calendars, photo books, slideshows and web albums.

It's part of iLife '08, the latest version of Apple's lifestyle software suite, which also includes iMovie, iDVD, iWeb and GarageBand.

iPhoto is easy to use but it's also very powerful. It displays all your photos in a single, searchable library, and can also organize them into individual albums. It can accommodate up to 250,000 photos, so the size of your photo collection is more likely to be limited by the amount of hard disk space you have available, not iPhoto itself.

9.2   How iPhoto works

iPhoto Library

Earlier versions of iPhoto imported your photos into an *iPhoto Library* folder in the *Pictures* folder on your Mac. iPhoto '08 now creates a single *Library* file, which is a little less confusing. This file contains the photos, keywords, editing adjustments, albums and everything else you create in iPhoto.

There is one option you should be aware of before you import large numbers of images, though. By default, these are copied into the iPhoto Library, so you'll end up with duplicates of your photos, which could fill up your hard disk prematurely. This is unlikely to be a problem with iMacs, which have big hard disks, but can be an issue with the Mac Mini or MacBook (though only if you have thousands of photos).

It is possible, though, to get iPhoto '08 to reference your existing photos in their current location. To do this, use the **iPhoto > Preferences** menu command. In the **Preferences** dialog, click the **Advanced** button. Now de-select the box labelled **Copy items to the iPhoto Library**.

iPhoto will still create a Library file, but this time it will simply keep a record of where the photos are located. In use, iPhoto will work in just the same way. The one thing you have to be careful about, though, is moving any of your photos later using the Finder, because iPhoto may lose track of where they are.

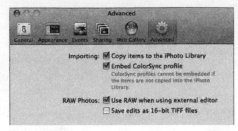

By default, iPhoto copies your pictures into your library, but you can set it to refer to them in their existing location.

9.3 Importing photos

There are two ways of importing photos into your Library. You can simply choose the one that makes most sense to you.

Import photos already on your hard disk

This assumes the photos have already been transferred from the digital camera. You can transfer photos from your camera to your Mac's hard disk either by connecting the camera to the Mac using the camera's USB cable, or by taking out the memory card and inserting it into a memory card reader plugged into the Mac. If you have installed the camera maker's software, it may attempt to transfer the pictures from the camera automatically. This isn't always a good thing because it may not always be obvious where the software is going to save the photos. It's best

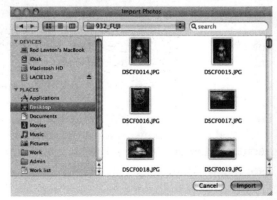

You can import photos which have already been copied from your camera on to your Mac's hard disk.

to plan your own system of folders for storing your photo collection, using the Finder. If you cancel any automatic download and then quit, you should find an icon for the camera on the desktop. You can double-click this icon to open it, double-click the folders inside, locate your photos and drag them across to your computer manually. Now you can start iPhoto, open the **File** menu, choose the **Import to Library** command, locate the photos and import them.

Import photos from your camera/memory card

To download photos directly from the camera, start iPhoto, then plug in your camera. iPhoto should detect your camera automatically and switch to Import view, ready to copy across the photos. If not, or you're importing pictures from a memory card reader, use the **File > Import to Library** command and look for the camera or memory card reader's icon on the Desktop.

If this is the route you want to follow, remember what we said earlier about the iPhoto preferences. Make sure iPhoto is copying the files into the Library. Otherwise, when you remove the card, iPhoto won't be able to locate them any more.

If you connect a digital camera while iPhoto is running it will detect it automatically and offer to import any photos on the camera.

The import process may take anything from a few seconds to several minutes, depending on the number of photos.

Once the import process is complete, you'll see your photos have been added to the Library as a new *event*. This is a new feature in iPhoto '08 – previously, photos were imported in *rolls*.

Events are Apple's attempt to simplify the way we browse ever-larger collections of photos. Each event is represented by an icon – but not an ordinary icon. If you move the mouse pointer from left to right across it, you'll see that you can skim through all the photos in the event, seeing what's there without actually having to open the event itself.

In iPhoto '08, sets of photos are automatically split into 'Events' when you import them.

9.4 Viewing and browsing photos

Now let's take a closer look at the iPhoto interface. Running vertically down the left-hand side of the screen is the **Source** list. At the top, in the *Library* section, you can click on **Events** to view your photos as Events, or **Photos** to view them as one long, continuous list.

Below this is the *Recent* section. This contains a button to display the **Last Import** (the batch you added most recently), **Flagged** images and a **Trash** icon.

Flagging is new to iPhoto '08. You might flag photos that you want to come back to later, or those that are going to need some enhancement, or pictures you want to consider for a photo book or web album. To flag a photo, click on it in the main window to select it and then click the **Flag** button at the bottom of the screen. When you click the **Flag** button in the Recent section of the panel on the left, all the photos you've flagged are displayed.

To delete a photo, select it and press [**Backspace**] to send it to the Trash. (Just like the Trash on the Desktop, this one doesn't get emptied until you say so, just in case you change your mind.)

When you create your first Album, a new *Album* section is added to the Source list, with your new album in it. Any Smart Albums (see Section 9.8) that you create are shown here, too.

Like other Mac applications, iPhoto uses a Sidebar, this time to display its photo Source list. This includes events and any albums you create.

9.5 Creating albums

You can browse through your photos using the events created automatically by iPhoto, but it's likely that you'll prefer to organize them manually, especially where you want to combine photos taken on different locations – you might want to create a *Birthdays* album, for example.

There are two ways to create an album:

♦ Select the photos you want in the main window. To select more than one, click on the first in a series and then [Shift]-click on the last to select both photos and all of those in between. Alternatively, where there are gaps between the photos you want, **[Command]-click** on each photo you want to select. Now drag the photos you've selected on to a blank area in the Source list. A brand new album is created with these photos, and its name is highlighted ready for you to type in a name of your own.

♦ Alternatively, start by creating the album using **File > New Album.** Now drag the photos you want into this album either individually or several at a time.

9.6 Using keywords and comments

You may find that albums provide you with all the organizational tools you need. Sometimes, though, you will find that photos don't fit neatly into a single Album, or that you forget which album contains the photo you want. This is where Keywords are useful.

Keywords are individual words or phrases which can be embedded in digital photos so that programs like iPhoto can search for particular images.

To display iPhoto's keywords, open the **Window** menu and choose the **Show Keywords** command (or use the **[Command]-[K]** shortcut). This is another feature that has changed in iPhoto '08 – previously, keywords were displayed in a panel in the bottom left-hand corner of the window.

The **Keywords** palette may already contain some keywords, depending on whether any of the pictures imported already had keywords assigned by another program. But you can add your own. To do this, click the **Edit Keywords** button at the bottom. Keywords can also be typed in directly below the photo in the main window.

In previous versions of iPhoto you could find pictures which had particular keywords by clicking the keyword in the panel. In iPhoto '08, the Keywords palette is just for keyword management. To search for photos you now use the unified Search box at the bottom of the window.

iPhoto's searches are amazingly fast, as you'll discover, but you may get more photos than you bargained for. How do you narrow down the search? Well, if you type more than one keyword into the Search box, iPhoto will only find photos that match both keywords.

Keywords aren't the only way to tag photos with information. You can also type in freeform comments using the **Info** panel displayed in the bottom left-hand corner. (If this isn't visible, click the 'i' button below the Source list.) Use the comments area to type in more detailed descriptions of your photos. When you use the Search box, iPhoto will also use these descriptions to help you find the photos you want.

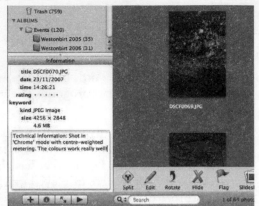

The Comments panel enables you to type in longer descriptions for individual photographs.

9.7 Using ratings

You'll notice that this Information panel also allows you to type in *star* ratings for photos between 1 and 5, and these can also be entered by clicking the row of star buttons below each photo in the main window. It's up to you how you choose to rate pictures, and whether you bother at all, but ratings can be useful later on as you try to pick out your very best photos from an ever-expanding library. For example, you could create an album for your last holiday and then rate each photo individually. Once you've done that, select the album to display your holiday shots, then open the **View** menu and choose the **Sort Photos** command and **Rating**.

If you want to see the star ratings underneath each photo, open the **View** menu and choose **My Rating**.

Ratings are also useful if you decide to use smart albums, which we'll be looking at next.

If you give your pictures star ratings you make it much easier to find your best ones later on.

9.8 Smart albums

Ordinary albums are a great way to organize your photos, but they require a good deal of manual upkeep. What if there was some way of getting iPhoto to create and maintain albums automatically? There is, and it's called *smart albums*.

Smart albums are automatically filled with photos that have specific properties. For example, you might want a smart album that displays all your holiday photos.

+ Before you start, set up any keywords that you will be using.

1 Open the **File** menu and choose **New Smart Album**.

2 Choose a name for the smart album and then adjust its search conditions. This sounds more technical than it is.

3 Using the pop-up menu, choose **Keyword** as the condition, and choose 'is' from the pop-up to its right. The third pop-up, far right, should now display the list of keywords applied to your photos and '*holiday*' should be amongst them.

This is a search criterion and it has three parts: the type of data you're looking for, whether it's an exact value or within a certain range, and what this data is.

This Smart Album picks out all the 5-star photos in a 'Trannie' event (photos shot on transparency film, just in case you're wondering...).

That's it. All done. The new smart album will automatically display all photos with the 'holiday' keyword. As long as you remember to add this keyword to all your holiday shots in future, the Smart Album will update automatically.

Smart Albums are smarter even than that, though. You can set up more than one condition (criterion) to narrow the conditions. For example, the second condition could be that the rating is 5 stars. Now the Album will only display your 5-star holiday shots. The other advantage of Smart Albums over the ordinary sort is that if in the future you decide to change the keywords or the ratings for some of your photos, any Smart Albums will, again, update automatically.

9.9 Editing photos

iPhoto is great for collecting and organizing photos, then, but what can it do about fixing up photo failures and generally enhancing your pictures?

To edit a photo, double-click it to open it in full-screen mode, or use the **Full screen** button in the bottom left-hand corner of the iPhoto window. In full screen mode, if you move the pointer to the bottom of the screen, a strip of image-editing controls will

iPhoto has a wide range of tools for enhancing photos and in the latest version, all these adjustments can be reversed later if need be.

appear. These include Rotate, Crop and Straighten tools, a quick-fix Enhance button, a Red-eye button and an Adjust button. If you click the Adjust button, this will display iPhoto's full set of image adjustment tools. They're surprisingly powerful and, in iPhoto '08, they work in a whole new way.

In previous versions, if you changed a photo, iPhoto would save the new version, but also keep the old one in case you needed to go back to it. In iPhoto '08, the original image is never actually modified. Instead, the changes you make are stored within iPhoto as a series of instructions. If you open the photo in future, the positions of the adjustment sliders are just as you left them, so that you can carry on changing your mind about how best to enhance a photo without ever committing yourself to permanent changes to the image. It's called *non-destructive* editing, and it's a new way of editing photos that's starting to appear in other programs, too.

9.10 Printing photos

Now collecting thousands of photos on your computer is a pretty dry and dusty pastime unless you find some way of sharing them with other people.

The simplest and most traditional method is to print them out, and there are lots of really good low-cost inkjet printers out there which can produce photographic prints every bit as good as those you'd get from a conventional photo lab.

To print a picture from within iPhoto, simply select it in the main window and press the **Print** button at the bottom. This displays a dialog where you can choose the print style from a list on the left (Standard, Contact Sheet, Framed). To the right is a preview of how the photo will look with the current settings. Below, though, is the important bit. You need to make sure the correct printer is selected and that the paper type, size and print quality are set correctly too.

With inkjet printers it's essential to use proper photo paper and to tell the printer that's what's being used. If you don't, the picture quality will be badly affected because the amount of ink the printer delivers must be tailored precisely to each paper type.

To output a photo, press the Print button and choose the page size and photo layout required.

9.11 Creating slideshows

The alternative to prints is a slideshow. At one time you wouldn't have thought about getting friends and family to gather round a computer screen, but with today's larger, higher-resolution displays – and particularly the excellent iMac displays – there's no reason not to. The chances are your computer's display is now not much smaller than the TV in the corner of the lounge.

Slideshows are easy to set up in iPhoto. It's best first of all, though, to create an album containing the pictures you want to show. Click the album to select it, then click the **Slideshow** button at the bottom of the screen. iPhoto will display the first picture and, underneath, a range of slideshow settings. You can have a lot of fun playing with the slide delay, the *Ken Burns* effect and even adding your own music track, but for now just press the **Play** button to get a feel for how it works.

Slideshows are the digital alternative to setting up a projector and screen. You can change the slide duration and the transition effect between slides.

9.12 Cards, books and calendars

To the right of the Slideshow button are buttons for creating books, calendars and cards. This is another way of sharing your photos, this time by turning them into personalized gift items. In each case you can choose a template and customize it with your own photos, messages and information. The options are really quite impressive... but how do you print these out?

You get the impression that these options have been designed with online printing services in mind. Many photo lab sites already offer gift items like these, and iPhoto is clearly tapping into this market. But you don't have to order books, calendars and cards online. You can print the pages on your own printer, if you like, and you might well want to do this if you're simply interested in trying these things out.

In the long run, getting gift items like these made commercially does make a certain amount of sense, particularly with photo books. You could print out the pages individually, but you wouldn't be able to bind them as effectively or as professionally as an online photo lab.

9.13 Creating web albums

iPhoto '08 can also publish your photos as web albums, and there are three ways of doing this: (a) by publishing them to a personal web gallery, though for this you need a .Mac account; (b) by sending them to the iWeb application that comes with the Mac; (c) by exporting simple web page layouts which you can then upload yourself to whatever web host you want to use.

These web galleries are like those you can create using Yahoo! and other sites with photo album features. But where Yahoo! and others let you choose and upload your photos from within your Internet browser, it's obviously an advantage to be able to do it from within iPhoto instead, if that's the tool you use to organize your pictures.

And this means you will need a web host of some description, whether it's one you choose yourself or a .Mac account.

.Mac accounts are the simplest option, but they're not free. Currently in the UK they come with an annual subscription of around £65. It might sound a lot if you're used to things on the Internet being free, but you do get a lot for your money, and you can find out more about .Mac and what it offers in Chapter 14.

One advantage of using the .Mac service is that creating a web gallery is easy. You just create and name an album to store the photos you want to include, select all the photos in the album and click the **Web Gallery** button at the bottom of the window. iPhoto uses the album name as the web gallery name and asks you who you want to be able to see the photos (the online Help explains the privacy settings). Now you click the **Publish** button. The photos are then uploaded to the web gallery (this may take a few minutes, depending on the number of photos). You can click a link to visit the published site when the upload is complete, and send an email inviting others to come and look at it, all within iPhoto.

There's more, though. When visitors take a look at your web gallery, what they get is not just another photo gallery website – it's a rich, interactive experience! Galleries can be viewed in four modes: Grid (an array of thumbnails), Mosaic (one big image with thumbnails alongside), Carousel (you move a slider to 'spin' photos through the viewer) and slideshow. Its also possible to adjust the settings so that friends and relatives can download the photos and even upload their own.

Web galleries published in this fashion are shown in iPhoto's source list so that you can examine them, add or remove photos and republish them as required.

We mentioned that you can also export sets of photos to iWeb, and this is done by selecting the photos and clicking the iWeb button at the bottom of the iPhoto window. You can then choose between two templates: *Photo Page* and *Blog*. This is a good route to follow if you've already used iWeb to set up your own web page and you want to integrate your photo albums with this.

Lastly, to export a simple web page which can be uploaded manually to another server, select the photos and use the **File > Export** command. This displays the **Export Photos** dialog, which has a *Web Page* section. Here you can choose the title of the web page, the number and size of the thumbnail images and the size of the photos themselves. This generates all the files needed for uploading and displaying the album. All you need now is instructions from your Internet service provider or web host on how and where the files should be uploaded.

iPhoto's online Web Galleries are quite stunning, though you can only create them if you have a .Mac account.

Summary

- iPhoto can import pictures into its own internal Library (the default) or simply 'reference' them where they are.

- Albums are useful for grouping pictures together for projects or slideshows.

- Keywords help you find pictures more easily.

- Comments are used for longer descriptions.

- Ratings give you another way to organize photos.

- Smart Albums use keywords and comments to find and display pictures automatically.

- Slideshows are a great way to share photos with others, particularly on today's large, high-resolution displays.

- iPhoto's web galleries look stunning, but you need a .Mac account to use them.

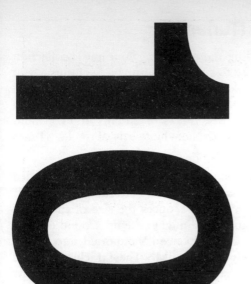

10 using iTunes

In this chapter you will learn:

- what iTunes can do
- how to copy audio CDs to your iTunes library
- where iTunes gets CD track information
- how to organize your music
- how to create playlists
- how to create audio CDs
- about iTunes and iPods
- about the iTunes store
- about podcasts
- about Internet radio

10.1 What is iTunes?

iTunes is a way of building and organizing your music collection on your Mac. If you want to hear a favourite piece of music, you no longer have to go looking for the CD it's stored on and find the right track on the CD. Instead, you can use the tools within iTunes to find specific artists, tracks or albums in an instant, even when your Library consists of thousands of tracks (iTunes calls them *songs*).

Your Mac can store thousands of tracks because they're recorded in a compressed format which doesn't noticeably affect their audio quality, but which greatly reduces the size of the music files. The music on an audio CD might take up around 600Mb of storage space on the CD, but once it's imported into iTunes the same tracks might only take up 60Mb. These tracks are stored in the *Music* folder (see Chapter 2 for more information on how and where files are stored on the Mac). If more than one person is using the Mac, then each user will have their own *Music* folder.

If you've used Windows Media Player on a PC, you'll find iTunes very similar in terms of what it does, even though it actually looks quite different. You can use iTunes to enjoy your music as is, using your Mac as a kind of hi-fi system (you can get plug-in speaker systems which provide excellent quality), or you can use it to create your own audio CD compilations – handy for the car, perhaps?

What's significant about iTunes is the way it's integrated with other Apple software. For example, if you're creating a presentation in Keynote, the presentations software in the iWork '08 suite, you can add an audio soundtrack directly from your iTunes library. Mostly, though, people use iTunes in conjunction with an iPod, creating *playlists* of favourite tracks in iTunes and then *synchronizing* them with the iPod so that they get to hear their favourite music on the move.

Music can be imported in one of two ways. The usual way is to copy it from audio CDs, but it is also possible to buy music digitally by paying for it and downloading it from the iTunes store. We'll look at the iTunes store later in this chapter, but for now we'll look at the way most people will get their music into iTunes – by copying it from CDs.

iTunes can store your whole music library on your Mac and find any track you want in an instant.

10.2 Copying CDs to your Library

Like many tasks on the Mac, importing an audio CD is so simple that it'll bring a smile to your face. Just insert the CD into the slot, wait a few moments for the Mac to mount the CD and you should find that iTunes starts automatically. It will then display a list of the tracks on the CD, together with the artist and album name, and to the left of each track is a checkbox with a tick in it. When you click the **Import CD** button at the bottom right of the iTunes window, it will import all the tracks which have been ticked – this is your opportunity, to de-select any tracks you don't want, although it's simpler to import them all and make up playlists later which contain only those you like listening to.

Wait a minute. How does iTunes know what all the tracks are called? This information isn't on the CD. Ah, but each CD sold has its own unique identifying code, and iTunes looks this code up on an online Gracenote database which carries track listings for every CD on sale. If you look carefully at the iTunes display while it's scanning the CD, you'll see it accessing this database.

This will only work, of course, if your Mac is connected to the Internet when you insert the CD. With a broadband connection, this will be on all the time, and the data will be retrieved automatically. If you're unable to connect to the Internet when you copy a CD, it's possible to look up track names later on when you do have a connection. First, select the track. Next, open the **Advanced** menu and choose **Get CD Track Names**.

If you copy a CD which isn't on the Gracenote database, you can type in track, artist and album names manually. To do this, click a name to select it, wait a moment, then click it again to make it editable (if your clicks are too close together, the Mac will interpret them as a double-click and simply start playing the track). Now use the information on the CD inlay to fill in the names.

In fact this is your chance to give something back to the world of music! Once you've finished entering the CD information, open the **Advanced** menu and choose **Submit CD Track Names** menu command to upload them to the Gracenote database.

Importing music is simple. When you insert a CD, iTunes looks up the album and track names on the Internet and offers to import them to your library.

10.3 Organizing your music

The iTunes interface can look a little daunting for first-timers. Where Windows Media Player puts on a very pretty face, iTunes looks like just what it is, a music database. But don't worry, it's all very straightforward. And before long you really start to appreciate this direct approach.

The iTunes window has two parts. On the left is a vertical Sidebar with a series of sections. These include:

> LIBRARY
> Music
> Movies
> TV Shows
> Podcasts ⑩
> Radio
> Ringtones
>
> STORE
> iTunes Store
> Purchased
>
> ▼ PLAYLISTS
> Party Shuffle
> 60's Music
> Music Videos
> My Top Rated
> Recently Played
> Top 25 Most Played
> Atom Heart Mother
> Be-Bop Deluxe: Axe Victim
> Beethoven
> Berlioz
> Bizet

* The **Library** section has entries for Music, Movies, TV Shows, Podcasts and Radio.

* The **Store**, which is the iTunes Store.

* Under **Devices** you'll find the currently inserted CD (if any) or an iPod, if you've got one connected.

* The **Playlists** section lists all the custom playlists you've created (collections of your favourite tracks) together with Smart Playlists, which are created automatically based on your ratings and other information. We'll look at Playlists in more detail in the next section, and some of the other items (Podcasts, Radio) at the end.

The point is that when you click any of the items in the Sidebar, you see all the relevant tracks in the main panel on the right. And it's the organization of these tracks and the way that they're displayed which we'll explain next.

To make things simpler, open the **View** menu and make sure all the items in the first section (Browser, Artwork, MiniStore, Equalizer and Visualizer) are *not* currently showing.

Now in the menu section below you'll see there are three choices: **List view**, **Album view** and **Cover Flow view**.

List view

In List view, the tracks are displayed in rows and the information for each – the Name, Time, Artist and so on – is arranged in columns. You can change the order in which they're displayed. For example, if you click on the *Album* column, the tracks will be arranged alphabetically by album name. See the little arrow to the right? You can click this to swap between Ascending (A–Z) and Descending order (Z–A).

So much for sorting tracks – but how do you find specific tracks out of a collection of thousands? Simply type the name (or an artist, or album name) into the Search box at the top right of the window. In an instant it will list the tracks, you're looking for.

Name	Time	Artist	Album
☑ Don Giovanni	6:49	Crudele – Non mi dir	Opera Gala
☑ Von Weber	3:50	Der Freischutz – Ko...	Opera Gala
☑ Von Weber	11:04	Der Freischutz – Ov...	Opera Gala
☑ Von Weber	2:52	Der Freischutz – W...	Opera Gala
☑ Wagner	8:03	Die Walküre – Act ...	Classic CD Issue 44
☑ Die Zauberflote	3:54	Dies Bildnis ist bez...	Opera Gala
☑ Madama Butterfly	3:02	Dovunque al mond...	Opera gala
☑ Le Nozze di Figaro	7:22	E Dusanna nom vie...	Opera Gala
☑ Madama Butterfly	1:05	Ed e bella la sposa?	Opera gala
☑ Otello –– Act 2, "Ora e per sempre addio"	2:26	Enrico Caruso	Classic CD 47
☑ Beethoven	7:35	Fidelio – Abscheuli...	Opera Gala
☑ Beethoven	10:28	Fidelio – Gott! Welc...	Opera Gala
☑ Beethoven	6:25	Fidelio – Overture	Opera Gala
☑ Jour a Jour – Anon	3:40	Gothic Voices	Classic CD – Disc 32
☑ Humperdinck	8:09	Hansel und Gretel ...	Opera Gala
☑ Budapest	10:05	Jethro Tull	Crest Of A Knave
☑ Teseo, Act 3 – finale, Sibillando	3:43	Jones (Medea); Les ...	Classic CD 29
☑ Requiem – Dies Irae; Tuba mirum	5:31	Konzertvereinigung ...	Classic CD Issue 42...
☑ Neon Lights	8:54	Kraftwerk	The Man Machine
☑ The Man Machine	5:32	Kraftwerk	The Man Machine
☑ Symphony No. 6 in E minor – first mov	8:29	London Symphony ...	Classic CD 29
☑ The Masses Against The Classes	3:24	Manic Street Preach...	Masses Against Th...
☑ Puccini	8:51	Manon Lescaut – O...	Opera Gala
☑ Chasing Sheep Is Best Left To Shepherds	2:35	Michael Nyman	The Draughtsman's...
☑ The Disposition Of The Linen	4:49	Michael Nyman	The Draughtsman's...
☑ Queen Of The Night	6:10	Michael Nyman	The Draughtsman's...
☑ Don Carlo –– Act 1, "E lui! desso l'infante!"	8:01	Michael Sylvester (...	Classic CD 36

In List view, your tracks are shown in a database-style table – the information in each track is shown in the different columns, and the more organized you are in putting details into this, the easier it will be to find tracks.

Album view

List view is the most useful for experienced iTunes users, but it may put many newcomers off because it looks like a database program. Album view is more logical for those who still think of their music in terms of the CDs it's stored on. Here, tracks are grouped by album, though this display format only really works if you have the album artwork too – an image of the album cover, in other words.

Artwork is available from the iTunes store, and is downloaded automatically if you buy music from the store. You can also download artwork for existing tracks from the iTunes store by opening the **Advanced** menu and choosing the **Get Album Artwork** command. However, this does require an iTunes account, which means supplying your credit card details in advance of any purchases you might make.

Album view will make the most sense to those used to sorting through a conventional CD collection.

Cover Flow view

This restriction also applies to the Cover Flow view. This is a very smart-looking display mode where you can flick through your albums (album artwork, that is) to find the album you want.

It is possible to add your own artwork to albums, but it means scanning in CD inlays or record sleeves, and it's more trouble than most of us are likely to want to go to. So unless you buy into the whole iTunes store idea, which is the place to get the artwork, you're better off using iTunes in its simple List view.

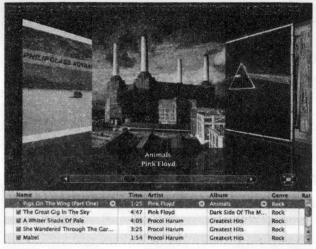

Name	Time	Artist	Album	Genre	Ra
Pigs On The Wing (Part One)	1:25	Pink Floyd	Animals	Rock	
☑ The Great Gig In The Sky	4:47	Pink Floyd	Dark Side Of The M...	Rock	
☑ A Whiter Shade Of Pale	4:05	Procol Harum	Greatest Hits	Rock	
☑ She Wandered Through The Gar...	3:25	Procol Harum	Greatest Hits	Rock	
☑ Mabel	1:54	Procol Harum	Greatest Hits	Rock	

In Cover Flow view you can spin through your CDs by dragging on the scrollbar underneath.

10.4 Creating playlists

We've explained how your music tracks are displayed and how you can sort them in the order you want and find specific tracks, but this isn't much use if you just want to sit back and listen to a few favourites played in a particular order. That's what playlists are for.

To create a playlist, click the '+' button in the bottom left-hand corner of the iTunes window. A new, 'untitled' playlist is created, ready for you to type in a name. Once you've done that, click **Music** in the **Library** section at the top of the panel. Now find the tracks you want in your Library either by sorting them by album or artist, or by using the **Search** box. Once you've found a track you want, just drag it on to the playlist. Do this with all the other tracks you want until your playlist is finished.

Now you can click the playlist title to display its contents in the main window. Is the order wrong? Just drag tracks up and down the list to change the order. Have you missed a track out? Go back to Music, find the track and drag it on to the playlist.

Playlists are useful when you want to listen to your favourite tracks on your Mac, but that's not all. They're also perfect for creating compilation audio CDs for playback on conventional CD players, and they're particularly useful when transferring music to an iPod. iPods don't have as large a storage capacity as your Mac, so you'll probably need to prune your music collection down to its bare essentials. What's more, you can't manage and organize music on your iPod – all the organization (like creating playlists) has to be done on the Mac.

Smart playlists

iTunes also offers smart playlists, and these can be a lot of fun, though they are far from essential.

Let's say you want a Wagner playlist but you can't be bothered to search through your whole Library for all your Wagnerian operas. First, open the **File** menu and choose the **New Smart Playlist** command. This displays a dialog where you can specify your smart search criteria. We could just choose *Artist* from the menu and type 'Wagner' into the box. It might work, but there will be many tracks where the artist is actually the performer and 'Wagner' may appear only in the track name, or even just the album title. To get round this you can add more search 'criteria' by clicking the '+' button to the right of the first one.

We won't go into any more detail here, but hopefully the idea is a little clearer now. And it'll become clearer still if you try a few Smart Playlist experiments of your own.

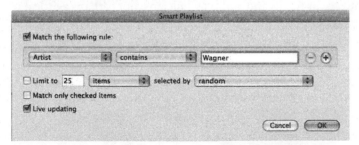

You can create playlists manually or you can create a Smart Playlist which automatically finds tracks by a particular composer, for example.

10.5 Enjoying your music

iTunes can be used to play music directly on your Mac, though it's likely that the built-in speakers won't provide the kind of hi-fi quality you're looking for.

The solution is straightforward, provided you have enough room on your desk and don't mind a few extra cables – get an accessory speaker set. These can be as simple as the inexpensive stereo speakers you buy for PCs. These are powered by their own mains adaptor and plug into the Mac's earphone socket.

More expensive speaker sets will provide better quality, right up to the standard you might expect from a modest hi-fi system. These consist of two stereo speaker units as usual, plus a 'subwoofer' for deeper, more powerful bass.

These aren't just useful for music. Many Mac users also use their computers to play back DVD movies, and a proper sound system will really enhance the experience, particularly if you have a Mac with one of the latest widescreen displays.

Whether you're using the Mac's built-in speakers or a sophisticated plug-in speaker system, it's possible to fine-tune the sound to match the capabilities of the speakers, the style of music you're listening to and your own preferences. iTunes has its own graphic equalizer, which you can display using the **View > Show Equalizer** command.

Like other graphic equalizers, this one enables you to adjust the strength of a whole series of different frequency bands. That's fine for hi-fi nuts and audio technicians, but perhaps a little daunting for the rest of us. But there is an easier solution – the Equal-

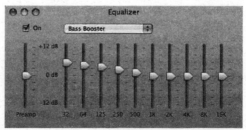

To get better playback quality, try tweaking the iTunes 'Equalizer'. For the best sound, though, you really need a good set of external speakers.

izer window also has a pop-up menu with preset adjustments for different speaker types and music styles. For example, if you're playing music using the built-in speakers in MacBooks, the *Small Speakers* setting is likely to give the best results. When you're experimenting with the different settings, do allow a few seconds for them to take effect – the changes aren't instantaneous, and this can fool you into thinking nothing has happened.

iTunes has one more trick for those moods when you just want to chill out and lose yourself in the music. If you use the **View** menu and **Turn On Visualizer** command, the iTunes window is taken over by randomly-generated patterns – although they're not truly random, since they respond to the music. The iTunes Visualizer might sound like a somewhat frivolous add-on, but actually it's quite fascinating to watch and can really draw you into the mood of the music.

You can also get the Visualizer to use the full screen. To do this, open the **iTunes** menus and choose **Preferences**, then click the **Advanced** tab of the Preferences dialog. At the bottom is the **Display visualizer full screen** option.

The Visualizer can also be activated using the **[Command]**-**[T]** shortcut. This also switches back to iTunes when you've had enough of watching those swirling patterns.

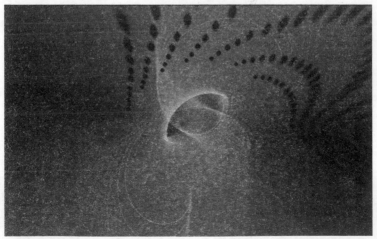

The iTunes Visualizer takes over your screen with patterns of light and colour which change in response to the music.

10.6 Creating audio CDs

One of the great things about iTunes is how easy it is to create audio CDs from tracks stored in your library.

Why would you want to do this, especially if you've just gone to the trouble of copying CDs to your library?

Well, CDs do have advantages. We mentioned one earlier – you might want to create some CDs to play back in your car stereo, or in a regular CD player. CDs are also a good way to back up any music you buy from the iTunes store, because until you do, they'll only exist as a digital file on your computer.

And one great advantage that your own CDs will have over the originals is that you can choose which tracks they contain, and the order they play in. After all, even our favourite artists can produce duds, and it's rare that we enjoy every single track on an album. In addition, with iTunes you can create your own 'best of' compilations using tracks from several different albums.

1 First, create a playlist containing the tracks you want to copy to the audio CD.

2 How do you know they will fit? Look at the bottom of the iTunes window when the playlist is selected. It will display the number of tracks (songs) and the total time.
Depending on the CD type, 1 hour is around the maximum.

3 With the playlist still selected (you should see its tracks in the main window), click the **Burn Disc** button in the bottom right-hand corner of the iTunes window.

4 A message in the status panel at the top flashes, saying 'Please insert a blank disc...' Slide a blank CD into 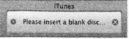 the Mac's CD/DVD drive. The display will now say 'Checking disc...' Then the burning process begins – iTunes writes the tracks to the CD. This will just take a minute or so and, at the end of the process, iTunes has generated an audio CD which is now ready to play in any regular CD player.

And that really is all there is to it.

10.7 Synchronizing with iPods

One of the key points about iTunes is that you don't need an iPod to make good use of it. You can use it to copy and enjoy your CD collection, download music from the iTunes Store and create your own compilation CDs, as we've seen.

However, for those who want to enjoy their music on the move, an iPod is the obvious choice, simply because they integrate so perfectly with iTunes.

Other portable music players do exist, of course, but it may not be so easy to transfer your music to these. By default, iTunes uses the AAC format for music files, which is not the same as the MP3 format used by most other devices.

iTunes can be configured, however, to copy music in the MP3 format instead. This is done using the iTunes Preferences and the **Advanced** tab. Here, you click the button for the **Importing** section, where there's a pop-up menu for changing the file format used.

Many third-party music players are compatible with iTunes, and will appear in the iTunes window as a device to which you can copy music. However, music downloaded from the iTunes store will only play on iPods and iTunes-compatible devices, which currently include certain mobile phones.

Needless to say, using an iPod with iTunes is very much simpler. When you connect the iPod, its icon will appear in iTunes, which will do one of two things, depending on how it's been set up: iTunes will automatically synchronize your Library with the iPod (the default), or you can opt to manage your music manually.

Automatic synchronization is the simplest choice because it takes care of all the file transfers for you. If you create a new playlist, copy a new CD or buy new tracks from the iTunes store, they're automatically copied to the iPod the next time you connect it. But this only works if the capacity of the iPod is large enough for your entire music Library. It won't be a problem with the larger iPod classics, which have built-in hard disk drives with capacities of 80Gb (enough for 20,000 tracks!) or more. With iPod Nanos, it's quite likely that your music Library will soon be too large to fit. This is when you need to swap to the Manual mode. To do this, you click the iPod's icon to display its **Summary** screen, and choose the appropriate **Options** at the bottom.

Incidentally, you might want to explore the other sections of this window, because you can also synchronize Podcasts, Photos and even Contacts from your Address Book to your iPod.

When you manage music manually, you transfer tracks to the iPod by first selecting the **Music** button in the Library section,

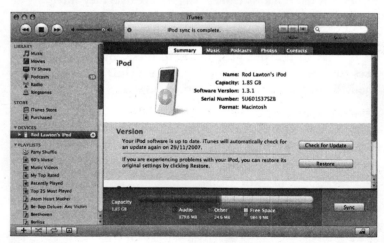

iTunes and iPods are designed to be used together so it's no surprise to learn that transferring tracks and even synchronizing your library is easy.

top left. Now you can select tracks from the main window and drag them on to the iPod icon, or drag Playlist icons on to it.

On the iPod, music is automatically sorted by artist, track and album name, so you can find the tracks you need that way – or, you can choose a playlist instead. Playlists are probably the best choice because it's not possible to change track orders on iPods – you can't program in your favourite tracks in the same way that you can in iTunes. Think of them simply as playback devices for music you've already organized in iTunes.

10.8 The iTunes store

Most readers will have noticed a trend away from conventional CDs towards music downloads. It's hard to predict right now whether this will ultimately spell the end of CDs, but that seems unlikely in the short term. Many consumers remain mistrustful of digital distribution and prefer the ownership of a real object (a CD) to a collection of digital files. However, music downloads do have many advantages, and for customers as well as distributors. For example, you can click the **iTunes Store** button in iTunes to access the iTunes Store via the Internet and search for specific tracks or albums which may be difficult to find in retail stores.

Now remember our remark earlier that you seldom enjoy all the tracks on an album? When you shop at the iTunes store, you can buy tracks individually (currently 79p in the UK), and this can work out cheaper for albums which contain just two or three classics (why pay for a whole bunch of others you don't really like?). Alternatively, you can buy the whole album – the price is listed, and it's easy enough to do the sums.

When you make a purchase, you don't get a CD sent to your house. It's not like buying from Amazon! Instead, the music is downloaded to your Mac when you make the transaction. These files are stored in your iTunes Library alongside your others. The album art (the cover) will also be downloaded and stored in iTunes to be displayed alongside the music you've bought.

It's a good idea at this point to burn a CD of your new purchase, just in case something happens to your Mac and you don't have any backups.

You can buy music from the iTunes store an album at a time or a track at a time, and it can all be done from within the iTunes window.

To buy from the iTunes Store you must set up an account, and this is where some buyers may be reluctant to proceed, as it means lodging your credit card details so that future transactions can be charged to your card automatically, although the Store will alert you to this and check that you want to proceed.

This will be a stumbling block for those who prefer transactions to be clear-cut, single payments. On the other hand, if you're prepared to accept the terms, costs and frequent uncertainties of a mobile phone contract, the iTunes Store is hardly any different. Indeed, it's far less likely you'll incur unexpected costs here. This is a payment method we may all have to get used to in the future as more and more companies seek to automate their payment services.

10.9 What's DRM?

We can't talk about downloads from the iTunes Store without talking about *DRM*, or *Digital Rights Management*. This is the music industry's attempt to protect music from unauthorized copying, which is perceived as a much greater problem now that music can be downloaded.

Currently, there are restrictions on the way downloaded music can be used. These are not imposed by Apple, but are requirements of the industry as a whole. These also apply with rival music download services – not just Apple. The iTunes Help and the iTunes Store list these restrictions. At the time of writing, they can be summarized as follows. Downloaded music can be:

* Played on up to five computers

* Synced with your iPod

* Synced with or streamed to your Apple TV

* Burned to audio CDs or DVDs (you can burn a song an unlimited number of times, and as part of a playlist up to seven times).

The commercial climate is changing though, and in response to public pressure there are signs of a shift back to unprotected music, and these are offered as *iTunes Plus* tracks at the iTunes Store. We won't go into any more detail about DRM versus iTunes Plus here because the situation is likely to change. The important thing is to be aware of the copyright issues involved and your own rights when you buy the music.

10.10 What are podcasts?

Podcast is this year's buzzword, just as *blog* was last year's. A Podcast is like a radio or a TV show you can download and play back via iTunes. Most are free, but some have to be paid for.

To see how it works, go to the iTunes Store (you don't need an account for this) and go to the *Podcasts* section, where you can browse sections devoted to Comedy, Sport, the Arts, News and Music. Podcasts are classified as video or audio and are illustrated with small images and brief descriptions. To find out more, you click on the image.

Here you'll find that most podcasts come in several instalments, or episodes, which are shown as a list. This list will also tell you whether they are free or not. You can download individual episodes, or *subscribe* to the podcast so that new episodes are downloaded to iTunes automatically.

Podcasts are submitted to the iTunes Store by many publishers, and the list of available podcasts is already so long that you could spend an awful lot of time just browsing through them.

Podcasts are video or audio 'programmes', often free, which can be downloaded to iTunes individually or subscribed to as a series.

10.11 What's Internet radio?

But podcasts aren't the only way to enjoy broadcasts with iTunes. For those brought up on radio rather than television, iTunes and the Internet breathe new life into this unique medium.

It's all done with *Internet radio*, which has been made much more practical by high-speed broadband communications. First, click **Radio** in the iTunes **Library** section. iTunes will now list a whole range of music genres, including jazz or reggae, for example. Each of these expands into a whole list of Internet radio stations. To try one, double-click its name. In a few moments, you'll be connected to the radio station's live audio stream.

Internet radio isn't limited by transmitters, aerials and reception. As a result, you can listen to radio stations all over the world, from Belgrade to Boston, without interference or atmospherics. (Internet radio isn't unique to iTunes – it's built into Windows Media Player on PCs, too.)

Music and video downloads tend to grab all the headlines these days and Internet radio is often overlooked. And that's a shame, because there are some great radio stations out there which provide constantly-changing background music and even introduce you to new artists and genres you might never have encountered if you'd stuck to the same old predictable favourites you know already.

It's not been possible in this chapter to fully explore everything that iTunes can do or examine in great depth those things we have covered. Hopefully, though, you now know enough to start exploring this exciting new world of digital entertainment on your own.

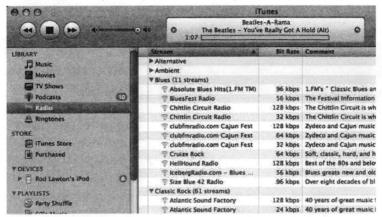

Who said radio is dead? Now you can listen to stations from around the world, and without a 40-foot mast in your garden.

Summary

- iTunes lets you store your music collection on your Mac.

- You can copy music from CDs or download it from the iTunes store.

- iTunes can be used on its own, or used to manage music on an iPod.

- Playlists let you choose tracks and the order they play in. They can also be used to make compilation CDs.

- Podcasts are like pre-recorded radio or TV shows you can download.

- Internet radio is a great way to listen to free radio stations around the world.

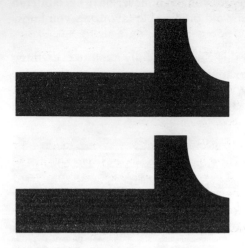

11

iMovie and iDVD

In this chapter you will learn:

- how to import video into iMovie
- how to organize and browse clips
- how to create projects
- how to add transitions
- how to add titles and voiceovers
- how to export finished movies
- how to create new iDVD projects
- where to find movie files
- how to change menu and title text
- what the Drop Zone is for
- how to burn a DVD

11.1 What iMovie does

iMovie and iDVD are both involved in the creation of movies, and it can be difficult to understand where one leaves off and the other takes over.

In this chapter, then, we'll try to explain the difference simply and get you started with both programs so that you've got a clearer idea which you need, when and why.

There's a lot more to both programs than we cover here. Our aim is not to provide a complete reference, but to explain the basic concepts so that you can understand what you're able to do and you know broadly how to do it. All the step-by-step details can be found in the online Help.

We'll start with iMovie. iMovie is to movie clips what iPhoto is to still photographs. You use iMovie to import and organize all your video clips, whether they were shot on a camcorder or a digital camera.

iMovie goes further. With digital photos you can compose shots carefully to leave out unwanted detail. It's no so easy with video clips. Unexpected things happen. The action you're waiting for may take too long to arrive. Many of your video clips will include long sections where nothing much is happening. That's

You can use iMovie to edit out the best bits from your video clips and combine them into professional movies.

why videos need editing before they're fit for showing to other people, and that's the other thing that iMovie does. You can edit your clips and combine them in Projects which can then be exported as polished, standalone movies.

Note that iMovie '08 is very different from the previous version. So different, in fact, that if iLife '08 is being installed as an upgrade, the older version of iMovie is retained for those who've got used to the way it does things. If you're buying a new Mac with iLife '08 already installed, this doesn't apply.

11.2 What iDVD does

The movies you create in iMovie can be played back on the Mac, uploaded to YouTube or emailed (if they're short enough) to your friends and relatives. But what if you want to create a movie on a DVD, one that will play back on a domestic DVD player?

Creating DVD movies, complete with titles and menus, requires special software – and that's what you need iDVD for. (You'll also need a Mac with a DVD writer – a superdrive.) Although it might appear that iDVD and iMovie do a similar job – adding titles, combining movie clips – they're actually very different. iMovie is for combining clips into single movie files. iDVD is for converting one or more movie files into a DVD.

iDVD enables you to create DVDs with menus using your own movie clips.

11.3   Getting clips into iMovie

First, we'll look at how to get movie clips into iMovie. These days there are a number of devices which can record video, including mobile phones. Here, though, we'll stick to the two most common: MiniDV camcorders and digital cameras.

To import video from a camcorder, first rewind the tape to where you want to start recording and connect it to the Mac using a Firewire cable (you may need to get this separately). Now look for the **Open Camera Import Window** button in the iMovie window (it's the button with a camcorder icon).

In the **Import** window, choose the camcorder from the pop-up menu in the bottom left-hand corner (if you have a MacBook or an iMac, this will also list the built-in iSight camera). You can now press the **Capture** button to start recording the camcorder footage. iMovie will ask you where you want to store it – the Movies folder is the most logical place. You'll also be asked whether you want to store it in an existing project or a new one. Projects are explained in the next section.

If your video's been shot on a digital camera or some other solid state storage device, it will have been saved as separate video files. To import these, open the **File** menu and choose **Import Movies**. You can then browse the contents of your Mac to find the video clips you want to import.

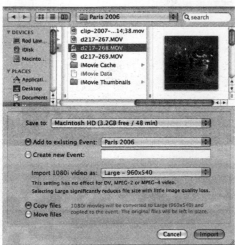

Movie clips recorded on digital cameras can be copied to your hard disk and imported from there. Footage from MiniDV camcorders can be imported using a Firewire cable.

11.4 Organizing and browsing clips

The iMovie window has three main areas: the Event Library, the Project Library and the Preview panel.

The Event Library is like the events display in iPhoto. Instead of displaying movie clips individually, iMovie groups them into these events. You can click on an event to see all the movie clips it contains. You might set up an event to contain all the clips you shot on holiday, for example.

These clips aren't displayed as single thumbnail images (like they were in the previous version of iMovie, for example). Instead, they're displayed as filmstrips containing a series of thumbnails taken from the video at five-second intervals. Why do it this way? It gives a clearer idea of the duration of a clip – longer clips produce longer filmstrips – and makes it easier to identify key points in the clip. If the five-second intervals produce too many thumbnails, use the slider in the bottom right-hand corner of the window to change the interval to ten seconds, say.

There's another slider in the top left-hand corner of the Event Library window. This is for changing the size of the thumbnails.

Now's the time to introduce iMovie '08's party trick. If you move the pointer over a clip, it plays back, and at the speed you're dragging the pointer. This makes it really easy to see what's happening in a clip and to skim to the points you want very quickly. As you move the mouse you'll see a vertical red bar moving across the clip. If you release the mouse, this bar stops at that point in the clip. Now, if you press the spacebar, the movie plays at normal speed from that point – press the spacebar again to stop it.

Video clips are shown as a filmstrip and you can 'skim' through the footage simply by moving the mouse across it from left to right.

11.5 Creating a project

As shot, movie clips tend to be rather raw. They need trimming and combining to produce a decent movie you'll be proud to show to others, and that's what the Project Library is for.

First, you use the '+' button at the bottom of the Project Library panel to create a project – you'll be prompted to choose between 4:3 and 16:9 aspect ratios. 4:3 is the ratio most camcorders and digital cameras shoot in by default; it's also that of traditional TV sets. Many camcorders and cameras can also shoot in the wider 16:9 ratio – the aspect ratio of today's widescreen TVs. Choose the ratio that matches the clips you'll use in the project.

Once the new project is created, you can drag clips on to it from the Event Library panel. Now this isn't quite as straightforward as simply dragging a thumbnail because moving the mouse pointer over a clip, as we saw earlier, plays back the clip. The alternative is to [Ctrl]-click the clip and choose **Select Entire Clip** from the menu. This places a yellow border around the whole clip and now you can drag it.

The Event Library is where you collect your raw video clips, but the Project Library is where you assemble them into movies.

But maybe you don't want the whole clip? Maybe you only want a part of it? In this case, move the red playback bar to the point in the clip where you want your selection to start and then drag until the end of the section you want. As you do this you'll see a yellow border pick out the section you've selected. You can now drag this selection to a project.

It's also possible to trim clips once they've been added to a project. Just select the section you want, open the **Edit** menu and choose **Trim to Selection**.

Once clips have been added to a project and you've trimmed them as necessary, you can rearrange them into the right order, ready for the next step...

11.6 Adding transitions

It's a bit unsubtle if one clip stops and another starts in the blink of an eye. *Transitions* are a standard movie technique for fading one scene into another. To add a transition between clips, click the **Transitions Browser** button in the bottom right-hand corner of the Project Library panel. A selection of pre-configured transitions appears in its own panel, and you can preview any of them by placing the mouse pointer over it. When you've found one you like, drag it from the Transitions panel and onto your project, positioning the mouse pointer carefully between the two clips you want to blend – they'll move apart slightly to make room for the transition.

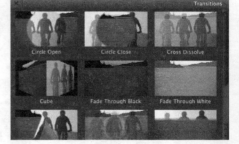

To add a transition just choose it from this panel and drag it between two clips in your project.

11.7 Adding titles

It doesn't look quite right, either, if your movie just starts, without any kind of introduction. This is where you need a Title screen and, again, you can add one using drag and drop. This time, click the **Titles** button in the bottom right corner of the Project Library. You'll see a selection of title layouts and, when you've found one you like drag it in front of the first clip in your project.

The Preview window will now show you the title screen and its dummy text. You need to type over this with your own text, and to do this, drag the mouse pointer over the text to select it and then type your own. And just to add that little finishing touch, why not add a transition between the title and the first clip?

Titles are added in the same way. This time, you choose the title you want and drag it in front of (or on to) the first clip before typing in your own text.

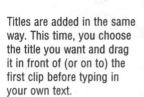

11.8 Adding a voiceover

Some of your clips will feature speech that hasn't come out too well, either because of wind noise or because the person speaking is too far away. Other clips desperately need some kind of commentary but don't have one. In both cases, the solution could be a voiceover added in iMovie. All you need is a Mac with a microphone.

First, you click the **Voiceover** button (the one with a picture of a microphone). Then you do what the message on the screen tells you to do – click on the clip you want to add the voiceover to. You get a three-second countdown, and then the microphone starts recording as the playbar starts moving over the clip. When you've said your piece, click the mouse to stop the recording.

Voiceovers don't replace any existing audio. Instead, the audio track that's already there is faded slightly and your voice commentary is added over it. When your commentary stops, the clip's audio is subtly faded back to its original volume.

This is what's so great about iMovie – it produces professional-looking results without any effort or know-how on your part. It does so much more, too, that we haven't been able to cover here, but which you'll enjoy discovering on your own now that you know how iMovie works.

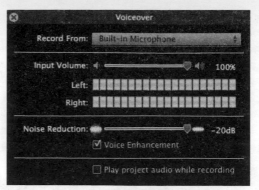

Cips with bad sound may benefit from a voiceover. iMovie uses the Mac's built-in microphone and subtly overlays the existing sound with your commentary.

11.9 Exporting the movie

That's not quite the end, though. At the moment, the movie project can only be played back in iMovie. To send the finished project to other people you have to export it as a movie file. To do this, open the **Share** menu, where you'll see a whole host of options. For example you can send the movie to iTunes, where it can by synced to an iPod. You can send it to YouTube, if that's your thing, you can publish it to the Mac's Media Browser so that it's available for dragging and dropping into documents created by other applications like Pages and Keynote, and you can send it to a .Mac Web Gallery if you have a .Mac account.

If you want to create a DVD, though, you need to choose the **Export Movie** option. You'll be prompted to choose a name for the movie, the location where you want to save it and the output size (choose pixel dimensions close to those of the original recording device). iMovie will now export a movie file which you can import into iDVD...

11.10 Creating a new iDVD project

iDVD is a simpler program than iMovie because it only has one job – to turn regular movie files into DVDs with menus which can be played, like commercially-available DVDs, on domestic DVD players. (Actually, iDVD can also produce photo slideshows and mix them with videos, but we'll keep it simple for now.)

When you start iDVD, it will open the last project you worked on (if any) or prompt you to create a new one. iDVD, like other Mac software, offers ready-to-use templates to make the job as easy as possible. iDVD has a selection of themes which are displayed vertically down the right-hand side of the window. Each theme has different screens, titled Main, Chapters and Extras. To get started, just choose the Main screen from one of these themes.

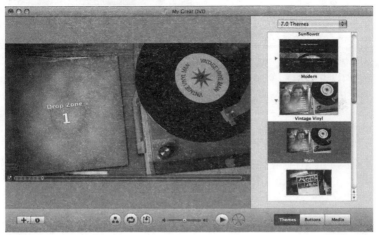

iDVD comes with a range of very attractive-looking project templates to make your DVDs look really professional.

11.11 Importing video

This screen will now appear in the main window, ready for you to add your own content. To do this, click the **Media** button in the bottom right-hand corner of the iDVD window and then click the **Movies** button top right to show the contents of your iMovie Event Library and the Movies folder.

All you have to do now is drag a movie clip from the Media window on to the Main screen (but not on to the Drop Zone area). When you do this, a button will be added, labelled with the filename of the video file.

Now carry on adding as many video files as you want. iDVD will build a movie menu on the screen.

As you add movies to your project, iDVD adds them to the screen as a menu.

11.12 Simple modifications

At the moment, the movies are labelled with their filenames, which isn't very helpful. To change this to something more meaningful, click the text once to select it and then again to make it editable. You can now type in a title of your own. You'll also notice that buttons appear directly below which let you change the font used and the size of the text.

That's not all you can do. We mentioned in the previous section that you shouldn't drop movies on to the Drop Zone area. This Drop Zone is for photos or movies which you want to play on the main screen while viewers are deciding which video clip to click on. You should choose something decorative or diverting rather than a clip which people need to pay attention to.

There's a lot more you can do with iDVD that's not covered here. The intention, though has been simply to get the basic principle across. The rest can be explored at your leisure – the online Help is very good, and there's a Getting Started PDF which you can print out and keep by your side as you experiment further with the features.

You can change the menu titles, and you can add photos or video clips to the 'Drop Zone' to personalize the menu page.

11.13   Burning a DVD

The final step in the process is to burn your DVD, and this option can be found on the **File** menu. iDVD is very helpful. It will check your project before it burns it and report any errors that you might want to attend to. You can also open a DVD map to check the structure of more complex DVDs, and use the Project Info dialog (from the **Project** menu) to check the space used and other technical information prior to burning the DVD.

Summary

* iMovie stores your video clips in its Event Library.

* Clips can be incorporated into Projects where they can be cut, combined and re-ordered.

* You can add transitions, titles and voiceovers without any specialized knowledge.

* Finished projects must be exported as movie files before they can be used in iDVD.

* iDVD's sole function is to produce DVDs with menus that play in domestic DVD players.

* DVDs are prepared using a range of pre-designed templates.

* Creating a DVD is simple, but there are many more advanced options for those who want to take it further.

12 organize your life with iCal

In this chapter you will learn:

- what iCal can do
- about the different calendars
- how to add an appointment or a To Do
- ways to remind yourself of upcoming events
- how to add a contact to your Address Book
- how to set up an email group
- about Smart Groups

12.1 What does iCal do?

iCal is a digital diary. You can use it to keep track of all your appointments, jobs, meetings and social events. It comes as standard with all Macs, and you'll find its icon on the Dock.

iCal is laid out like a calendar, and there are buttons at the top to let you switch between Day, Week and Month views. Either side of these buttons are arrows for going backwards and forwards in time. iCal has a Sidebar, just like other Apple applications. This one has a list of *calendars*. Calendars are used to organize your appointments into *work* and *personal* items, for example, or to hep you manage different projects.

Depending on how iCal was set up when it was last used, there may be other items on the screen. In the bottom left-hand corner are three buttons: **Add a New Calendar**, **View or Hide Mini-Month** and **View or Hide Notifications**. These open a small panel in the bottom left which displays additional information.

Notifications are used when working alongside other iCal users, to request and organize meetings. The Mini-Month display can be useful for moving forward or backwards weeks or months at a time. We'll look at calendars shortly.

iCal acts as a digital diary with day, week or month views and can also keep track of your To Do list.

In the bottom right-hand corner of the window is a thumb tack button. This is used to show or hide your To Do list. When the To Do list is displayed, the main calendar display shrinks slightly to make room for it.

12.2 Creating an appointment

To create an appointment:

1   Use the buttons to move to the day you want to create it on (click the **Today** button to go straight to the current date).

2   Use the mouse pointer to drag out an appointment over the time slot you want it to cover. You'll see a new event appear as you drag the mouse. When you release the mouse button, the 'New Event' text is already highlighted ready for you to type in your own title.

3   You can move this event if you need to, and alter its duration. To move it to a different time slot, or even a different day, just drag the event with the mouse. To change its start time or end time, move the mouse pointer over the top or bottom edge and then drag that edge up or down.

12.3   Setting a reminder

How many times do you jot down an appointment and then forget all about it? With iCal you can set up reminders to give your memory a jog ahead of time.

To do this, double-click the event you want to be reminded about. This opens a window where you can change its properties – we're interested in the alarm setting roughly half-way down. By default, the alarm is set to *None*, but if you click the pop-up menu you'll see there are other options. The most useful are *Message* and *Email*. If you choose *Message*, iCal will display a reminder in a dialog on the screen. If you choose *Email*, iCal will send you a reminder by email.

Worried you might forget what you've got to do? iCal can display an alert on the screen or send you an email reminder.

In both cases you can choose how many minutes, hours or days ahead of the event you get the reminder – you can also choose a specific date for the reminder. If you select an email reminder, you can specify the address the reminder is sent to (this is useful if you have more than one email address, and perhaps one that you use when you're away from the office, for example).

The event dialog also lets you change the date(s) for the event – this is useful if you want to move it to a date outside the current view. You can set it to be an all day event instead of occurring at a specific time, and you can also choose the calendar the event belongs to. We'll look at calendars next.

12.4 Using multiple calendars

Do you keep one diary for work and one for home? In iCal you can separate these different aspects of your life by using different calendars within iCal. You can create as many as you like. To start with, you might find just a single calendar is all you need – it's certainly the least confusing setup to begin with.

Calendars, as we saw earlier, are listed in the Sidebar to the left of the iCal window.

* To create a new calendar, use the button at the bottom left of the window.

* To change a calendar's name, just double-click it and type in the new name.

* To change a calendar's colour-coding, select it and use the [Command]-[I] shortcut to open its info panel. The colour pop-up is in the top right-hand corner.

Each event you create is assigned to one of these calendars, and it shows up in that calendar's colour. These calendars do more than provide a quick colour-coding system, though. Do you see the checkboxes to the left of the calendar names? To hide a calendar, un-check its box. To show it again, re-check the box. In this way, you can choose exactly which events are displayed, and this can make it easier to plan and schedule.

If you only want to see one calendar out of several, it's a bit laborious de-selecting them all one-by-one, but there is a quicker way. Hold down [**Command**] as you click on any calendar's checkbox – this will hide them all. Now you just click the box for the calendar you want to see.

These colour-coded calendars look very pretty and do allow a lot of flexibility, but it's easy to get seduced by the novelty and set up lots of calendars you don't really need. You may find that you waste too much time assigning events to the correct calendars, and that a single calendar is both simpler and a lot quicker to work with.

12.5 Adding a To Do

As well as handling events, iCal can track all those jobs you know you've got to do at some point, but which don't require specific time slots. Like renewing your car insurance, for example, or organizing tickets for a business trip.

To create a To Do, first display the **To Do** list using the button in the bottom right-hand corner of the iCal window. A new To Do appears with its title already highlighted ready for you to type in your own. Note that new To Dos are always assigned to the currently selected calendar. If you select the calendar before you create a To Do (or an event, for that matter), it saves having to choose the calendar later.

New To Dos created in this way don't have a specific completion date. They stay on your list of To Dos for ever until they're done – when they are, click the checkbox to the left of the To Do. This indicates to iCal that the job's been done and it disappears from the list.

To Dos can simply be left floating, or they can be given a specific completion date, a priority and an alarm so that you don't forget them!

To set a deadline (completion date) for a To Do, double-click it to open its info window. Here, you check the **Due date** box, whereupon the palette produces a date display where you can enter the date you want and, below that, is an option to send yourself a reminder (alarm) – these work like event reminders.

You'll see from this window that you can also set a **Priority** of **Low, Medium** or **High**. This can be useful if your To Do list is very long and you're self-disciplined enough to approach it in a systematic, methodical fashion. At the top of the To Do list is a **To Do Items** pop-up which lets you sort your To Dos by **Due Date** or **Priority**.

You might decide the only way to get a To Do done is to assign it a timeslot. To do this, just drag a To Do onto the calendar display to create a new event, adjusting its duration, start time and date as necessary. Similarly, you might decide that you need to prepare items or carry out certain tasks in advance of a forthcoming event. In which case, drag the event on to the To Do list, and choose a suitable title and due date for the new To Do.

12.6   Viewing your To Dos in Mail

One of the new features in Mail is the ability to enter To Dos. These are the same To Dos you see in iCal, even though the screen layout is different. When you create a new To Do in iCal, it appears in Mail, and vice versa.

This brings the Mac into line with Entourage, the personal information manager and email program supplied with the Mac version of Microsoft Office, and with Microsoft Outlook on the PC. People want their calendars, address books and email all linked together, and that's what the Mac now does.

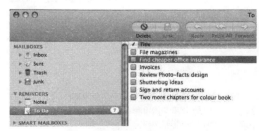

To Dos you create in iCal appear in Mail, and vice versa.

12.7 What does Address Book do?

iCal takes care of events and To Dos, Mail takes care of your email messages (and To Dos) and both link to Address Book, the third in the Mac's trio of personal information management tools.

At a basic level, Address Book is simply a repository for all the email addresses you need in Mail. When you receive an email message you can click the sender's name to display a pop-up menu with the option to save their details to your Address Book. To send an email, you enter the recipient's name or nickname in the **To:** field and Mail will use the Address Book to look up their full email address.

Address Book can also be opened and used on its own – you'll find its icon on the Dock. The window has three vertical panels for groups, names and contact details respectively.

Let's say you want to add a phone number or an address for one of your contacts.

1 Type their name into the search box, top right – this is the quickest way to find people once your list goes beyond a couple of dozen entries.

2 Address Book will list all the matching names – select the one you want, to display the contact information to the right.

3 Click the **Edit** button at the bottom. It's now possible to modify and add contact information.

4 When you've finished, click the **Edit** button again.

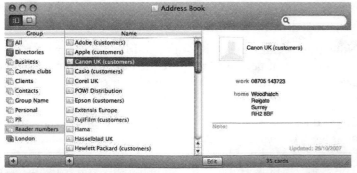

Address Book isn't just for email addresses. You can use it to store phone numbers, postal addresses and more.

Address Book isn't just an accessory for the Mail program, then, but a useful standalone program for looking up phone numbers, street addresses and even notes about individuals. This can prove useful at work for jotting down information about business contacts, and at home when you're building a list of things to get your partner for his or her birthday!

You'll note that Address Book can store multiple phone numbers, including mobile and fax numbers, and even the names of friends or assistants. See the green '+' and red '-' buttons? You can use these to add or remove phone numbers or email addresses, and use the pop-up menus alongside to indicate whether they're for work or home.

12.8   Organizing contacts into groups

But what about these *groups*? Well, sometimes you want to send the same message to lots of different people at once. It may be necessary to send out a regular bulletin to members of your team at work, or you may be the secretary of a club or society, with the job of keeping members up to date on what's happening.

1   Create a new group using the '+' button in the bottom left-hand corner and give it a name.

2   You can add people to this group by first clicking **All** at the top of the *Group* column and either scrolling through the list of contacts on the right or using the search box to find specific individuals.

3   When you've found a contact who needs to be added to the group, drag them from the *Name* column on to that group.

Now groups can be useful within Address Book for narrowing down the list of people to those related to work, home or other areas of your life. But they come into their own when you need to send bulk emails.

To do this, instead of typing the name of an individual into the message's **To:** field, open Address Book so that its window is in front of the Mail window, then drag a group into the **To:** field. This is a very powerful feature, so make sure you really do want to send the message to all these people!

12.9 New: Smart Groups

iPhoto has smart albums, the Finder has smart folders, and Address Book has smart groups. It's a new feature which could be easily overlooked by those who don't know it's there.

Like the Smart tools in other Apple programs, smart groups display contacts whose details match certain specific criteria that you specify.

As an example, let's say we want a group that contains all our contacts who live or work in London. We know that this is indicated by telephone numbers that begin with '0207' or '0208', so this can be our smart group criterion. (We could also do this based on postcodes, but while we have telephone numbers for all these people, we don't have all their addresses.)

1 Choose **New Smart Group** from the **File** menu and give a name to the group – we're calling ours *London*.

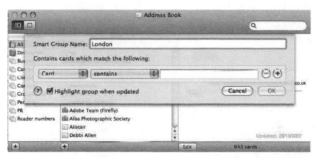

2 Now choose the criteria for the group. We set the first pop-up to **Phone** because it's phone numbers we're looking for. The next pop-up is set to **begins with** and in the third box we type '0207' as the London area code.

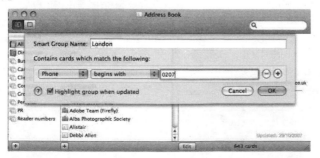

3 Some London numbers start with '0208', though, so we need to click the '+' button to the right of the first criterion to add another one. For this second criterion, we repeat the steps we took for the first, but this time type '0208' in the box.

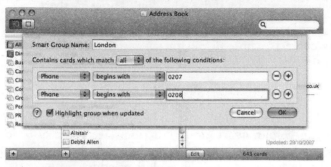

4 Now these Smart tools can work in two ways. They can be used to search for items which match all the criteria, or for items which match any of them. It's a crucial difference. In this case, we're looking for 0207 or 0208 numbers, so we need to set the pop-up above the search criteria to *any* rather than *all*.

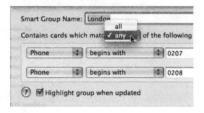

There's much more to Address Book and the way it can be used with other Mac applications than we've had the space to explain here, but hopefully we've helped you get started at least. Between them iCal, Mail and Address book can really help you get your life organized. But if you find it all too much fuss, don't despair. Some of us still get on much better using nothing more sophisticated than a pen and paper. Just because your Mac can do all these things, it doesn't mean you have to go along with it. Computers are there to assist our way of working, not define it!

Summary

+ iCal can act as your digital diary.

+ You can set up different calendars for work, home and other areas of your life.

+ iCal can also keep a To Do list of jobs to be completed.

+ With Leopard, your To Do list can now be viewed and edited in Mail, too.

+ Address Book isn't just a repository for email addresses – it stores phone numbers and street addresses too.

+ Address Book can be used to set up Group emails.

+ The Smart Groups in Address Book collect related contacts together automatically.

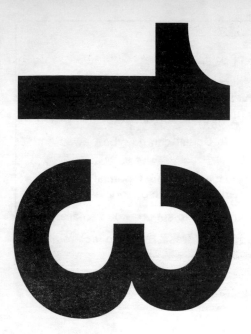

13

get online with iWeb

In this chapter you will learn:

- how to create your first website
- how to type in your own website content
- how to add objects to web pages
- how to create websites with multiple pages
- the difference between a website and a blog
- how to set up a blog
- how to get your website online

13.1 Getting started

iWeb enables you to create attractive-looking websites easily, using ready-made templates supplied with the program.

When it's started for the first time, iWeb prompts you to create a site and choose a template. After that, it opens to display this website and any others you create in the program window.

This window consists of a main panel which displays the web page currently being worked on, while at the left is a Sidebar which lists all the websites you've created and the pages within them. Each web page is displayed as a heading with a 'globe' icon, and alongside it is a drop-down arrow which is used to 'expand' or 'collapse' the list of pages in the website.

It's possible to create many different web pages within a website, or just stick to one, depending on what you want the website to do. To begin with, it's probably best to stick to a single page to get an idea of how iWeb works.

1 Choose **New Site** from the **File** menu. This displays a dialog with a list of website templates on the left. You click on one of these templates to see a list of page designs on the right.

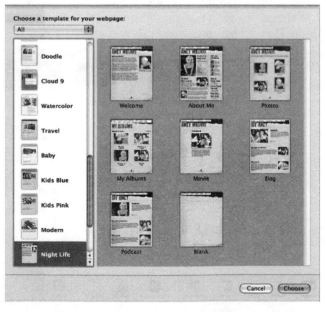

2 Let's say we choose the *Night Life* template and the *About Me* page design. iWeb now displays this page in the main window. You'll notice that it's also created a new *Site* in the sidebar and an *About Me* page within that site.

3 Make sure the *About Me* page is selected. Whichever page is highlighted in the Sidebar is displayed in the main window. What if you change your mind about the design? Click the pop-up **Theme** button underneath and choose a new design.

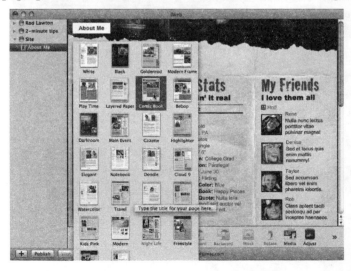

13.2 Adding your own text

iWeb's page templates look like finished pages, but the intention is, of course, that you replace what's there with your own information. (Most users find it less daunting to start with a finished page which they adapt rather than a blank sheet they have to fill from scratch.) Let's start by changing the name on the About Me page. To do this, click on it (you may have to click twice – once to select the box the text is in, and once to select the text). This is *placeholder* text – it's designed to be typed over, so a single click selects a line or paragraph at a time. It's the same with all the text on the page. To change it, select it and type. The templates and text boxes are flexible, so that if you type more text than was there before, other objects move to make space.

Sometimes, when you're typing text into a smaller box – a heading, for example – the text flows on to another line and overlaps objects below. To fix this, click outside the box to deselect the text, then click the box once to select it. Text boxes have handles on the corners and edges. You can drag these handles to change the size of the box, or drag the centre of the box to change its position on the page.

To change the text's size, colour or font, click the **Fonts** button in the bottom right-hand corner of the iWeb window. Unless you've got a particular reason to change them, though, it's best to leave the text styles alone because they've been carefully designed to tie in together as part of the overall design theme.

13.3 Adding your own photos

Most of the iWeb page templates contain photos and these, again, are 'placeholders' which simply show you what the finished page can look like. You can replace a photo in one of two ways:

1 If you know where it's stored on your Mac's hard disk, open a Finder window, locate the photo and simply drag its icon on to the existing placeholder photo on the web page. The picture will be scaled to fit the space automatically.

2 Click the **Media** button on the toolbar at the bottom of the iWeb window. This opens a palette showing the contents of your iPhoto library (see how well these Apple programs work together?). You can use this to find the photo you want and drag it on to the web page.

13.4 Adding other objects

It's possible to do much more than just modifying objects that are already on the web page. You can delete existing template items, move them around and insert extra objects of your own.

- **To delete an object,** click on it once to select it and hit **[Backspace].**

- **To duplicate an object** (let's say you want another text box), select it and use the **[Command]-[D]** shortcut.

To create a new text box, click the **Text Box** button on the toolbar. iWeb creates a new, empty text box – it's not always obvious on some of the busier web page designs, so look closely.

To add a photo, open a Finder window or the Media palette as before, and drag it on to the web page. You can change the size of the photo by dragging its handles.

As you work with objects on web pages, you'll notice horizontal or vertical blue lines flashing up on the screen now and again. These are *smart guides* which help you align objects with others by *snapping* them into position. This helps the web page look better organized and more professional.

You can have a lot of fun experimenting with iWeb's different themes, customizing the text and graphics and adding your own web page content.

There's lots more to learn about text, photos and arranging web pages, but it's easy enough to pick that up as you go along with the assistance of the online Help. For now, we're going to concentrate on another important aspect of web design – building websites with more than one page.

13.5 Building a website

A website with a single page may be enough for telling other people about yourself, but most people will want to set up extra pages to cover different topics. That's why there are several page layouts in iWeb for each design theme.

1 To add a page, choose **New Page** from the **File** menu. This displays the template window you saw when you first created the site. Note that you can mix pages from different design themes in your website. It's possible, but it's not recommended! It might be colourful, but it will also look rather crass and amateurish.

2 Let's say you've already got an *About Me* page. Maybe you want to start a blog (there's more on blogs in the next section). To do this, choose the *Blog* template.

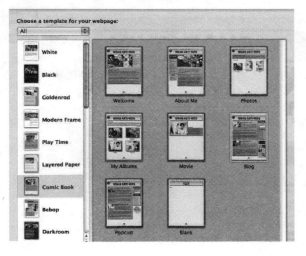

3 The Sidebar now displays the new page underneath the first under your Site heading. (Actually, blogs are a special case because they have more than one page, but we'll come to that in a moment.)

4 Something else has happened. You may have noticed that the original page had a small **About Me** button in the top left-hand corner. Now, there are two buttons: **About Me**
and **Blog**. When the website is published online, these buttons act as links to these pages so that you can easily jump from one page to another.

What iWeb is doing here is creating a *navigation bar* automatically. Every time a page is added to the site, it's also added to the navigation bar. This makes life a lot easier for you as you build the site, and for other people when they visit it.

There are other ways of linking the pages on your site – or of adding links to pages elsewhere on the Internet.

The About Me page has a *links* section already, in the bottom right-hand corner. At the moment, these links are dead – they're examples only, and not connected to anything. Setting up a link, though, is easy:

1 Create and/or select the text which is to form the hyperlink. This can be the web address itself, or just the name of the site.

2 Open the **Insert** menu, choose **Hyperlink** then select **Webpage** from the sub-menu.

3 This displays the Link Inspector, where you type the URL (Internet address) of the page you want to link to.

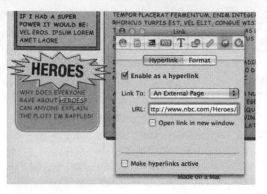

13.6 Websites versus blogs

Unless you've been living in a cave for the past couple of years, you'll be aware that blogs are the Internet's Big Thing right now. You're no one if you don't have a blog, and blogs – if we are to believe what we hear – are proof of the democratic power of the Internet and how the smallest individual now has as big a voice as the largest multinational.

What few people actually attempt to do, though, is explain what a blog actually is, so here goes...

Regular web pages are designed largely as static reference sources. The pages are written and published and visited by people who want to read them. Now and again, the information may need updating, and the pages are then rewritten and republished. It's like a book which is on the shelves for a certain amount of time then, after a while, updated and republished as a new edition.

Blogs are different. Blogs are like diaries, or journals. The point of a diary is not just what it says today, but what it said yesterday, and the day before and so on. They're fascinating because they give a glimpse back in time. It can add an extra dimension to an unfolding news story, or to your own opinions over time.

Many topical stories are revealed in a more interesting way by blogs. What's interesting is the way the facts, the journalist's own understanding and general public opinion change over time.

Most news stories are two-dimensional, whether they're on a printed page or a website. In a blog, they become three-dimensional.

It's not just journalists who write blogs. If you help run a club, a blog is a much better way of keeping in touch with your members, partly because they can look up information in back issues of your blog and partly because adding new blog entries is easier than continually updating a regular website.

Blogs are simpler than websites in some ways and more complicated in others. They're simpler in that each new blog entry is generally just a single page which is written to a template and, with practice, can be produced quite quickly. But they're more complicated in another sense because each blog entry is moved to an archive when the next one is added. Visitors to the blog can not only read the current blog entry but search all the archived entries for information too.

That's why Blog pages in iWeb look more complicated in the Sidebar. Each page has two sub-items: *Entries* and *Archive*.

With iWeb you can use a conventional web page as an introduction to one or more blogs. Blogs are like online journals, and are both easier to maintain and more digestible for visitors than big websites.

The Entries page is where you do most of your work. This is split into a conventional web page display at the bottom and a list of entries at the top. To begin with, there's only one entry – the one you're working on. When you want to add another, click the **Add Entry** button beneath the list. The previous entry then becomes part of the Archive.

Here's a tip. If you use the Add Entry button, iWeb adds another template page and you'll have to type in your own headings and add your own pictures all over again. To avoid this, customize the blog page template once, and then duplicate this entry (press [**Command**]-[**D**]) to create a new one.

You can also click the Archive page in the Sidebar to edit it in the main window. You don't see all your previous blog entries here because those are managed automatically online. Instead, you simply see the archive page *furniture*, and this is what you can modify.

Blogs in iWeb are much easier to understand once you start working on them. And for those with a .Mac account, they're really simple to set up and maintain.

13.7   Going live

There are two ways of publishing your finished website. If you have a .Mac account, all you have to do is click the **Publish** button in the bottom left-hand corner of the iWeb window. The .Mac account details will already have been set up, and iWeb now handles the upload process automatically.

When it's completed, iWeb will display the new web address for you. You can also visit published pages from within iWeb by first selecting the page in the Sidebar and then clicking the **Visit** button below.

iWeb is set up to work seamlessly with a .Mac account, as you might expect, and while many users in the UK might baulk at the prospect of having to pay an annual subscription when they're used to getting web services for nothing, in this case .Mac is so useful – not just within iWeb – that it really is worth considering.

If you don't have a .Mac account, it's still possible to get your websites online:

1 Instead of clicking the **Publish** button, click the Site in the Sidebar to select it, open the **File** menu and choose **Publish to a Folder**. You can now navigate to a folder or create a new one where all the files needed for the site will be saved.

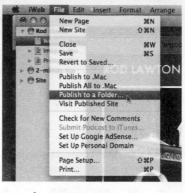

2 You'll need some online webspace for storing your site – most Internet accounts come with free web space, so check with your provider. They will also be able to tell you the address to send your files to, and the username and password to use, together with any other relevant technical information. To upload the files, you'll need a program called an *FTP client*. There are free or trial versions available online, and while FTP clients are generally straightforward, they can also be quite technical.

Summary

◆ iWeb contains ready-made web page templates to make website creation easier.

◆ You can modify the text and pictures already on templates and add new objects as required.

◆ When you add new pages to your site, iWeb adds them to the site's navigation bar automatically.

◆ You can create many separate websites.

◆ Blogs are like online journals – you constantly add new entries and old ones go to form an archive.

◆ iWeb works best with a .Mac account, but you can publish websites to a folder and upload them to another Internet host.

14 subscribing to .Mac

In this chapter you will learn:

- what the .Mac service offers
- how iPhoto web galleries work
- the advantages of a .Mac email account
- how .Mac makes creating websites simple
- how the iDisk is like a 10Gb virtual disk drive
- how .Mac can synchronize data between computers

14.1   What is .Mac?

Apple's .Mac service is an extended set of online services available to Mac users for an annual subscription. The cost (around £65 in the UK) might prove a sticking point for anyone accustomed to getting web services for nothing, but .Mac is a little different from most free web tools.

*   First, it's not cluttered up with ads (these are what pay the bills for other providers).

*   Second, it does things no other web services do.

*   Third, it integrates seamlessly with the Mac OS and its applications in ways we're about to describe.

And you can check these features out for yourself using the 30-day free trial that can be activated via the .Mac website, at www.apple.com/dotmac.

.Mac (dot.mac) is a subscription-based Internet service which extends the Mac's capabilities with a variety of useful online tools.

14.2   iPhoto web galleries

A little ahead of Leopard, Apple launched it's suite of iLife '08 applications. These can be bought as an upgrade package for Mac users with older versions, but they're supplied as standard on new Macs running Leopard.

And some of the biggest changes in iLife apply to iPhoto – not just in the way the application itself works, but in the ways you can now publish your photos online in galleries. Online photo galleries aren't new. You can already publish them – and for nothing – with Yahoo!, Google or a host of other web providers. The difference with .Mac, though, is the simplicity of the album creation and upload process, and the display quality and interaction available to those visiting your libraries.

Let's say you want to turn an album of holiday snaps into an online gallery. All you have to do is click the **Web Album** button on the toolbar at the bottom of the iPhoto window. There's no need to configure any Internet addresses or passwords because your .Mac account details are stored as part of your Mac's system settings. You're asked whether you want the pictures to be visible to anyone, to you alone or selected people (you can set up a list). The photos are then uploaded in the background and an alert tells you when the process has finished.

Your photo galleries can be viewed online using a Mac or a PC, and they're much more sophisticated than any free gallery alternatives. Photos can be displayed in a grid view with variable thumbnail sizes, you can skim through photos in an album without actually having to open the album fully, and – if you want them to – other people can add their own photos to the album, which synchronizes automatically with iPhoto on your Mac.

.Mac's web galleries look fantastic and integrate seamlessly with iPhoto. Publishing a gallery really is as simple as pressing a button.

Will you use these features? The simplicity of the upload process and the rich interactivity of the albums might convince you.

14.3 Email

The chances are you already have an email address provided by your broadband supplier, so why would you want another?

Email accounts come in two types. With a regular POP account, emails are downloaded to your computer when you connect. This keeps your mail private, but it has the disadvantage that your email account and your messages are locked in to that computer. What if you want to check your emails on a hotel computer, or in someone else's office? That's where *webmail*, or *IMAP* accounts are useful. Here, the mail is kept on a web server at all times, and you simply visit the server using any browser to check and reply to your mail.

.Mac email combines both so that mail is downloaded to your Mac but is also accessible online via a web browser. This is not unique. It doesn't offer any convincing technical advantages over other webmail services from Yahoo!, Google and others. On the other hand, a .Mac mail account does integrate perfectly with the Mac's Mail application and, again, it's free from ads.

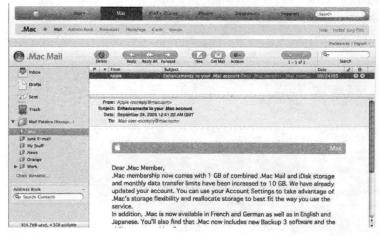

There are plenty of other free email services besides Mac Mail, but it does integrate perfectly with Mail and you can check your mail using a web browser.

14.4 Website publishing

Sooner or later you'll want to publish your own web page. It might be part of a college project, a way of keeping in touch with friends and relatives, or a bid for your own 15 minutes of Internet fame.

The Mac, of course, comes with iWeb, which was explored in more detail in Chapter 13, and you can use iWeb to publish web pages and blogs direct to your .Mac account. In fact, it works better this way. You can design a website, export it to a folder and then upload it to another web server run by a different company, but you may not get all of the features that the .Mac server offers. This applies if you want to set up and run a blog, too.

Of course, the more people who subscribe to a .Mac account, the more money Apple makes, so you could argue that it's in their interest to make sure that the .Mac hosted websites work better or are easier to design than those hosted by other companies. Even so, it is exceptionally easy to create websites and blogs with a .Mac account, and that ease of use has got to be worth a certain amount of anyone's cash.

iWeb is not the only web publishing tool available, though. The .Mac package also includes *Homepage*, which enables you to design web pages online using Safari rather than with a program

If you don't want to use iWeb to design your web pages, you can create them online using .Mac's homepage templates.

installed on your Mac. Homepage consists of a set of website design templates which enable you to build good-looking sites quickly. To a degree, Homepage looks and feels like a bit of a throwback to the previous generation of Apple site design tools (Homepage was a Desktop application on Macs a few years ago), but it's still useful for those who've yet to get to grips with iWeb. You can use it to make files available to others for downloading via a *File Sharing* page to which you can apply password protection if necessary. ('File sharing' is Apple's term to describe the way files can be made available to others – it's nothing to do with illegal music downloads.) This is ideal for authors or photographers who want to supply files to clients which are too big for email attachments (the files, not the clients).

14.5   iDisk

Your web pages, galleries, files and emails are all stored on your own personal *iDisk*. This is like a virtual disk drive stored on a .Mac server. The capacity has recently been upgraded to 10Gb, which is more than enough for the average user, though it's also possible to increase the capacity further for an additional charge.

Most Internet providers offer a certain amount of free web space, but normally to examine its contents you need an *FTP* program. As ever, though, Apple's found a simpler system for iDisk. It has its own icon on the Finder Sidebar, and its contents can be examined in the Finder just like those of any regular folder or disk drive. The access takes a little longer because it's happening over an Internet connection, but that's the only real difference.

It's possible to use iDisk like a second disk drive for transporting files you want to be able to access elsewhere, or for uploading them so that they can be made available on any File Sharing sites you set up. Some of the storage space on the iDisk is set aside automatically for other .Mac services and software downloads, which include an *iDisk Utility* which makes your iDisk available from a PC running Windows. In fact, an iDisk is like having a shared public folder online – you can make files available to others, and they can upload files to your public folder (it can all be password-controlled to restrict access, too).

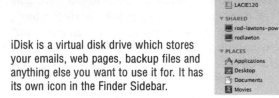

iDisk is a virtual disk drive which stores your emails, web pages, backup files and anything else you want to use it for. It has its own icon in the Finder Sidebar.

14.6 Synchronization

The iDisk has a multitude of uses. It can be a way of synchronizing emails, addresses, calendars and other information between different Macs, acting as a kind of online go-between. This is hardly essential for those using a single computer, but for anyone who has a Mac at the office and uses a MacBook when on the move, it could be extremely useful. These synchronization options are visible in the .Mac section of the System Preferences. You can choose what information is synchronized and when.

You can use the .Mac System Preferences to synchronize contact, calendar, address information and more with .Mac and other Mac computers.

The Preferences panel has another, very interesting tab called **Back to My Mac**. When this is enabled, it's possible to connect to another Mac over the Internet and via a secure connection to access files on that Mac and even to control it remotely. For this to work, of course, the other Mac must be left on all the time, and must have an always on Internet connection such as a company network or broadband. This feature might be useful to those who frequently have to work on the road and can't always predict what information they'll need to take with them. It's not very green to leave another computer switched on all the time, but it's a feature that might prove very useful to some.

14.7 Is it worth it?

There's quite a lot more to .Mac that we haven't covered here, and which is explained on the www.apple.com/dotmac site in some depth, such as .Mac Groups and using iDisk for online backups. All of these things can be tried out using the free 30-day trial.

The key question, though, is whether it's worth it? You may have a better idea of this after you've taken the trial. There are many advantages to a .Mac account that aren't immediately obvious, and which you may only appreciate weeks or even months later when the need suddenly arises.

At the same time, many Mac owners don't have .Mac accounts and never will. The point is that the Mac doesn't actually need the .Mac service – it's an excellent computer without it.

If you object to the very idea of paying an annual fee, notice how the whole media industry is moving towards subscription services. We may be used to getting our TV channels sent to us free over the airwaves, or websites offering information or services for nothing. Increasingly, though, we're starting to pay for premium or specialized content, like satellite or cable TV packages, or combined broadband/TV/phone deals. And we all stump up large amounts of money each month for mobile phone charges without a second thought. In this context, the £65 annual charge for a .Mac account isn't that high when it's compared with the convenience it can bring to many of your daily activities.

Is it worth it? It's certainly worth trying out and, even if you only find some aspects directly useful straight away, that in itself is probably enough to justify the cost of signing up properly.

Summary

- The .Mac service has an annual subscription charge of around £65 in the UK.

- It integrates with many Mac applications, including iWeb, iPhoto and more.

- Critics might complain of the cost, but the convenience and simplicity are undeniable.

- You can sign up for a 30-day free trial.

15 Dashboard widgets

In this chapter you will learn:

- about the Dashboard
- what widgets are
- about the widgets which come with the Mac
- how to hide the widgets you don't want
- where to find many more widgets online
- how to download and install them

15.1 What are Dashboard widgets?

That's a very good question! Widgets are like mini-applications which you can use for a whole range of jobs, from checking the definition of a word, to carrying out a quick calculation, to idling away a few spare minutes with a retro puzzle game. Widgets aren't opened like ordinary applications. They become visible only when you click the Dashboard icon on the Dock. All your widgets now become visible at once. Individually, they don't take up much space, and you can drag them around the screen into an arrangement which suits you.

It's easier to show what widgets do, than it is to try to explain them. We'll start with those that are supplied as standard. What we need to do, though, is split them into international widgets that are useful to UK users and US-only widgets which can safely be disabled as being of little use in the UK. The widgets that come with the Mac are of mixed usefulness, and you'll probably want to disable many of them. But there are many more widgets available online, and some of these really are remarkably clever.

First, though, let's deal with the standard widgets.

Address Book

This is just a small search box where you can type in the name of the person you want to look up in the Address Book. You may find it quicker than starting the Address Book application. Even as you're typing a name, the widget is listing matching contacts. When you click on a contact in the list, the widget displays the contact information.

Calculator

Need to work out the VAT on an invoice or the fuel consumption of your car? There's nothing fancy about this on-screen calculator, but it saves you having to rummage around in your desk drawers for a real one.

Dictionary

Need to know what a word means?
Type it in and hit [Return] to get a
definition, or choose **Thesaurus**
from the pop-up menu to find other
words with similar meanings.

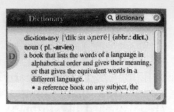

Google

You can run a Google search using
the search box in Safari, or you can do it here. When you press
[Return], Safari launches to show the Google search results.

iCal

In its standard form, this just displays
the current date and a mini-calendar.
But if you click the date it expands to
show upcoming events for the current
day. Click on an event to launch iCal.

iTunes

This is a mini-console for iTunes, though
given that iTunes has to be running for it
to work, it's questionable how much use it
is or how much time it saves.

Stickies

A yellow sticky pad you can use to jot down
notes. You can change the font and the pad
colour if you want to, but this is no word processor and its value, frankly, is limited.

Tile Game

Like the sliding tile games sold as novelties in toy
stores – you have to assemble the picture properly
by moving the squares around.

Translation

This one is very clever. It has two halves – in the top you type the word in English and in a few moments the translation appears in the bottom in the language you choose from the pop-up menu.

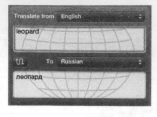

Unit Converter

Need to know how many pounds in a kilogram, or 65° F in Celsius? The Unit Converter has different sections for different types of conversion

(area, weight and so on) and could prove quite useful.

Weather

It's easy enough to get a weather forecast from the television or online, but this saves you the trouble with a six-day forecast which uses icons to illustrate the expected

weather graphically. Choose the nearest city to you by flipping the widget with its 'i' icon to show the settings on the back. Most locations are in the US, but it does have British cities too.

World Clock

You can use this clock to display the time in any city in the world. Useful, maybe, if you regularly speak to colleagues overseas.

US-only widgets

Business

This is an American service similar to Yellow Pages in the UK. As such it's not really any use to Mac owners in the UK.

ESPN

Another American service, this time devoted to the latest US football, hockey, baseball and basketball results.

Flight Tracker

An airline flight-finding service that unfortunately doesn't work in the UK.

Movies

This one can find films playing in cinemas across the US.

People

This is the American equivalent of the residential phone book in the UK.

Ski Report

Weather reports for the ski resort of Heavenly in California, anyone?

Stocks

You choose the stocks you want to follow by clicking the 'info' icon to spin round the widget and choose companies on the back.

15.2 Configuring widgets

There are two aspects to configuring widgets. The first is how you adjust the widget's settings – we've already mentioned this once or twice. Nearly all widgets have a small 'i' icon, usually in the bottom right-hand corner. When you click this the widget is spun round to show the back, where these settings are made.

But you'll also want to decide which widgets are displayed and to get rid of those which you don't want.

1 If the Dashboard isn't visible already, click its icon on the Dock. You'll now see all your widgets appear on the screen and your other applications will fade into the background.

2 With the Dashboard active, if you look in the bottom left-hand corner of the screen you'll see a large round button with a '+' symbol in the middle. You need to click this...

3 This opens up a horizontal *widget bar* at the bottom of the screen. This lists all the widgets currently installed on the Mac and not just the ones which are currently visible.

4 To display any of these widgets, click their icon in this bar. If you don't see the widget you want, use the arrow buttons at either end of the tray to scroll left or right to see more.

5 You'll note that in this mode each widget visible on the screen has a round '+' button in the top left-hand corner. To get rid of a widget, click this button to close it. It's not deleted from the system – it's still there on the tray – but it's not displayed on the screen any more.

6 To remove widgets from the widget bar, click the **Manage Widgets** button near the tray's top left-hand corner. All your widgets are now displayed in a list, and you can click the checkbox alongside any widget to deselect it and remove it from the widget bar.

7 Widgets can be deleted completely by clicking the red button to their right in this list. You can only do this with widgets you've down-

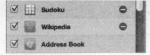

loaded and installed yourself, though, and we look at these in the next section.

15.3 Where to get more

The widgets supplied as standard with the Mac are a bit of a mixed bunch, but they are just the tip of the iceberg. Many, many more can be downloaded from the Apple website. They come from a whole range of sources, from big companies to self-taught programmers working from a bedroom. And while some are highly-specialized, others can be brilliantly useful, entertaining and inventive.

To find and install more widgets:

1 Open the **Manage Widgets** dialog (see step 6 above), and click the **More Widgets** button. This takes you to Apple's widget website. Or, start Safari and type the link into the Address Bar – **www.apple.com/downloads/dashboard**.

2 Ignore the **All Downloads** list on the left. Instead, look for the row of links under the **Dashboard Widgets** heading and click **Categories**.

3 Let's say you want to check out some games. Click the *Games* category to see a list of games widgets which runs, incidentally, over several pages.

4 To view more about a widget, click its title. You'll see a short description and find out whether it is freeware or a shareware/demo release. Most are freeware – free to download and use. Some are shareware, which means they run in trial mode for a while but later you'll have to pay to carry on using them.

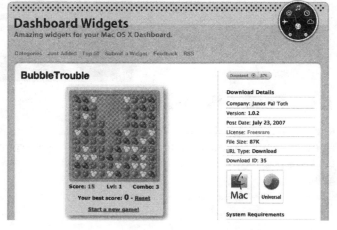

5 When you find a widget you want, click the **Download** button. Safari's Downloads window will show the download in progress, though widget files are very small and the download will be finished almost as soon as it's started.

6 When it's completed you'll be asked if you want to install the widget and open it in Dashboard – click the **Install** button.

7 You now get to try out the widget before pressing the **Delete** or **Keep** button. If you keep it, it's added to your list of widgets.

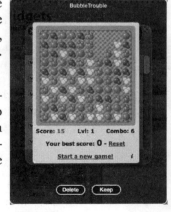

Searching for widgets is so absorbing, and the widgets themselves so simple and inventive, that you can spend hour after hour doing nothing but trying them out – you have been warned!

15.4 Favourite widgets

Here are four of the author's favourite widgets. These are just a few of the many thousands out there, so these are only examples of what's possible, not a definitive list of the only ones worth having.

CodeBreaker

A version of the classic puzzle where one player lines up a row of pegs of different colours and the other has to guess what they are with a series of guesses that gradually narrow down the options. Here, the Mac creates the code and you make the guesses.

Depth of field Calculator (DOFC)

A widget for photographers who want to calculate the depth of field (near to far sharpness) in a photograph. Highly technical, but to those who need it, a tool which sidetracks a lot of tedious calculations or complicated tables.

Sudoku

The classic number puzzle which has sold a million paperbacks can now be played on your Mac desktop. It's perhaps not quite the same as scratching away with a pencil in your favourite armchair, but it's great for addicts.

Wikipedia

The Wikipedia website is a great place to look up information on any subject, but this lets you do it without having to start Safari and navigate to the Wikipedia site. Articles are displayed in the widget window, which can be expanded if necessary.

Summary

* Widgets are mini-applications that carry out a host of useful little tasks.

* They're displayed by clicking the Dashboard icon in the Dock.

* Many of the widgets supplied with the Mac are designed for the US market, but they can easily be hidden.

* There are thousands of widgets which can be downloaded, and most of them are free.

* Widget files are small, so they're quick to download and take up little space on your Mac.

* Widgets can prove an endless source of fascination. Apart from useful everyday utilities, you can also download addictive and challenging little games.

16

games and utilities

In this chapter you will learn:

- about games for the Mac
- where you can get them from
- how to download game demos
- how to find and play games online
- how to preview electronic documents
- how to compress files for storage or emailing
- what you can do with Stickies
- things you can do with Photo Booth

16.1   Game types and top sellers

You don't normally buy a Mac just to play games. Serious gamers would invest either in a PC with an expensive and powerful graphics card or a dedicated games console like the PlayStation 3 or Xbox 360.

Having said that, there are more games available on the Mac than you might think, and some up-to-date best-selling titles too. You won't see them much in the shops because dealers concentrate heavily on the most common formats and don't usually devote shelf space to minority computers. But Mac games are widely available online if you shop at www.amazon.co.uk, for example. Do make sure you check the system requirements first, to make sure that your Mac has the hardware needed to run the game – and in particular that it has the right graphics card.

You may have already tried out the Chess game on the Mac, and the selection of Big Band board games. These, though, are just the start. So what kind of games can you buy for your Mac?

Combat games

These usually consist of first-person action (you see the game through the combatant's eyes) and a series of missions which you have to complete, or a more strategic approach to battle-fields where you make command decisions instead. Some games combine elements of both.

These games can be both involving and addictive. Examples include *Medal of Honor* (excellent first-person combat combined with suspense and tactics), *Call of Duty* (equally highly regarded) and *Quake* (18 only).

Mac games are hard to find in the shops but you can get them from big online retailers like Amazon, including the excellent Medal of Honor.

Simulating life

Here, you're attempting to run a game world using a set of complex rules which mirror those in real life. You can either have missions where you must reach certain goals, or you set your own goals and try to achieve them.

Sim City was one of the earliest *Sim* games but it has spawned many sequels. It's very complex and involving, though perhaps a little dry for those looking for a little light entertainment. If that is what you want, *The Sims* is a better bet. Here, you control cartoon characters in a cartoon world, trying to improve their careers and even their relationships. It's like practice for real life (almost)!

The Sims series is great fun and lets you mimic real life in the comfort and safety of your own home!

Driving games

Modern computer hardware has made a big difference to driving games, and examples in this genre include the excellent *Colin McRae Rally* and *Need for Speed*, though, admittedly, there aren't as many Mac driving games as there are strategy/wargames (though kids might like to try out *Disney Pixar Cars*).

You can emulate the late, great Colin McRae on your Mac, though admittedly there aren't that many good driving games.

Sports and other games

Fancy a round of golf? Then try *Tiger Woods PGA Tour 2005*, or *Madden NFL 08*. Many Mac games don't fall into any specific category, such as those spawned from best-selling films and a whole range of puzzle and board games.

You can practise your swing on your Mac, though you have to go right back to PGA 2005 for help from Tiger Woods.

16.2   Where to get Mac games

www.amazon.co.uk and other online software retailers are a good place to get Mac games, but you can also find out what's available by visiting **www.apple.com/uk/games**. Here you can find out about the latest games releases and discover whether games which are famous on the PC are also available in Mac versions.

Many games are made available as downloadable demos, and while the file sizes can be very large, with a broadband account they will still download quite quickly. To find out what's available, go to **www.apple.com/uk/downloads/macosx**. You should see a list of categories on the left where you can select *Games*. This heading now expands to show a list of sub-genres, so just click on the one you're interested in (*Action & Adventure*, for example). Now you can look through page after page of games, clicking on anything that looks interesting to get a short description and a screenshot. These games are a mixture of full commercial releases being distributed in a demo form, shareware games from smaller companies who distribute their software online rather than as boxed retail software, and some freeware games written just for the fun of it by amateur programmers.

And don't forget the Mac's ever-growing supply of widgets (see Chapter 15). Widgets are mostly free, and there's a huge range of games to try. Obviously these aren't going to be as elaborate as a full-scale commercial game, but they can still be very absorbing and entertaining nonetheless.

Looking for Mac games? Go to www.amazon.co.uk and type 'Mac games' into the search box.

16.3 Games online

It's also worth checking out a relatively new Internet phenomenon – online games sites. Here, you can choose from a wide range of comparatively simple yet very addictive games you play within your web browser window.

Anyone with school-age children should simply ask them which are the best sites because news travels fast in the classroom! **www.gamesgames.com** is a good place to start – again, you can select a genre from the list and click on any games which look interesting.

Here, you have to wait a minute or so while the game loads, and you will find that the standard of game varies considerably, to say the least. Having said that, the choice is huge, and if you persevere it won't take you long to find something that has you hooked.

These games are free. Sites like this are funded by ads, and while that is a bit of a nuisance, most of us soon become blind to them anyway.

Online games won't win any prizes for technical sophistication, but they're free, play on any computer and can be horribly addictive.

16.4 Mac utilities

The Mac comes with a number of utilities, which you can think of as software designed to do general odd jobs. We won't cover all of them here because many are highly technical and may never be used.

Preview

This is an application which the Mac uses to display image files when you double-click them in the Finder. You can zoom in to check for sharpness or even double-click several images and display them as a slideshow.

Preview also opens PDF files, doing the same job as the Adobe Acrobat Reader. Many manufacturers supply manuals as PDF files on CDs that come with the product, rather than providing printed manuals (electronic manuals are a lot cheaper). Here, Preview displays the document pages in the main window and thumbnail versions of the pages in a panel on the right to help you go quickly to the page you want. There's also a search box for finding specific text within the document.

The Preview utility is Apple's alternative to Adobe Reader, and you use it to read electronic documents and manuals in the PDF format.

Compressed .zip files

This isn't a utility as such, but a feature built into the Mac OS. On Windows computers you commonly compress a whole series of files into a single zip file to make it easier to email them to someone else. On the Mac, to do the same thing: select all the files you want to zip, hold down [Ctrl] and click on any of the highlighted files – then choose **Compress xxx items** from the menu. This produces a compressed zip file which other Mac users can open to retrieve the files. These zip files can be opened on PCs, too.

Disk Utility

This can be found in the *Utilities* subfolder in the *Applications* folder. You can use it to check and repair disks which appear to be giving problems, and also to erase (format) disks to wipe them clean. Disk Utility can also *partition* disks so that they appear and behave like different disk drives in the Finder (the total capacity will be the same as the physical disk itself). Partitioning is used when setting up a Mac to run Windows with Boot Camp.

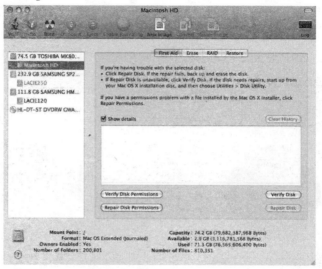

Disk Utility helps you repair disk faults, format disks and 'partition them' (for when you use Boot Camp, for example).

Stickies

The Stickies widget can also be found in the *Applications* folder. It displays sticky notes on-screen which work in just the same way as the real thing, only you don't get sticky marks on the screen and they don't fall off in hot weather. You can change the size of a sticky by dragging on its bottom right-hand corner, and you can create as many new stickies as you like. The contents of stickies are saved when you quit the program and reappear the next time you use it. You can also export the text of a sticky note (or copy and paste it) for use in another program.

Photo Booth

This is a harmless bit of fun for those with Macs that have an iSight camera built into the display. When you start Photo Booth, what you see is your own face staring at the computer. You can use Photo Booth to save snapshots of yourself and other users, either for fun or to add mugshots when setting up user accounts, for example. It's also possible to record video clips, and save both these and still photos to iPhoto or send them to other people by email. There are some special distortion effects you can apply too, and it's amazing how much puerile fun you and your friends can have with such a simple tool.

Photo Booth uses the camera built into the display of many Mac models. Use it to grabs stills or videos and have some fun with the special effects.

Summary

- There aren't as many games for the Mac as there are for the PC, but many big-name releases do come in Mac versions.

- The Apple website is a good place to go to learn more about games and download demos.

- Many websites offer free online games which you can play in Safari.

- The Mac's Preview utility does the same job as Adobe's Acrobat Reader.

- You can compress files into a single .zip file which Windows PCs can open.

- The Stickies application offers the digital equivalent of sticky notes.

- Photo Booth can take photo and video snapshots.

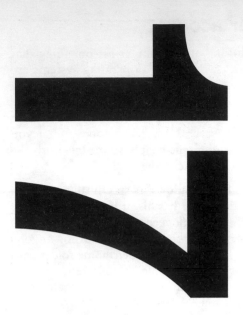

17 multiple users

In this chapter you will learn:

- what a user account is
- how to password-protect a Mac
- the advantages of individual user accounts
- how users' files are kept private and separate
- how one user can swap files with another
- how to enable fast switching

17.1   Your user account

You may be used to thinking of a computer as something that simply starts up and works, but today's operating systems are designed with multiple users in mind, and with protecting the privacy of each of these users. You may be the only person in the house or office who uses your Mac, but in most homes a single computer may be used by several different people. What you don't want is for all these different people to meddle with the settings and poke around with each other's files.

That's why the Mac OS, like Windows, is specifically set up to cater for multiple users. Each user has his or her own username and password, and when they've logged on it's as if the Mac is theirs. They see only their own *home* folder and not anyone else's and, by the same token, the files in their home folder cannot be seen by others. It's also possible for different users to choose their own desktop pattern and other Mac preferences without affecting those of other users.

You may not need to set up multiple accounts. You may indeed be the only person using your Mac. Nevertheless, it's important to understand that this system exists because it means that certain Mac features and jargon will then make sense.

For a start, you have a user account on your Mac, even if you are the only user. You can see this if you open the System Preferences and choose *Accounts* in the **System** section. The account will be under your name and labelled *Admin*. This means that you have *Administrator* privileges for changing settings on the Mac. You can do anything you like, in other words.

It's not essential to enter a password for this account, but it is a good idea, because even if your Mac is ever lost or stolen it will provide a certain basic level of security that won't stop a skilled hacker but would probably defeat a casual thief. But this will not work if the Mac is set for *Automatic Login*. This is the simple but lazy option! When the Mac is set up for Automatic Login, it'll start up without demanding your password. It's a nuisance to have to type this in each time you start your Mac, but it's a worthwhile precaution, especially with a portable MacBook or MacBook Pro.

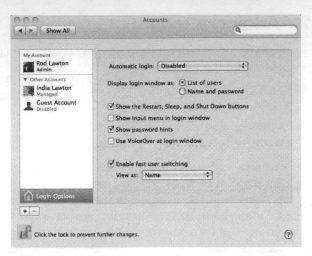

If you want to password-protect your Mac, go to Accounts in System Preferences and disable the Automatic login within the Login Options.

This option can be found in the **Accounts** panel – you click the account name on the left to select it, and then click the **Login Options** button below (you may need to click the padlock icon in the bottom left-hand corner of the window to unlock the settings). Now just make sure the Automatic Login pop-up shows **Disabled**.

To set or change a password, go back to the Accounts panel and click the **Change Password** button. You'll need to type in the old password (if any) before you're allowed to do this, and you're required to type in the new password a second time to make sure the spelling is consistent. If you forget your password you won't be able to start your Mac, but there is a failsafe mechanism built in – a *password hint*. Here you type a word or phrase that will jog your memory in the future and, if you do forget your password, you'll be able to look up this password hint from the Login window.

Now while you were in the Accounts window back there, you'll probably have spotted that you can set up additional accounts using the '+' button in the bottom left-hand corner. This is ideal if other family members need to use the computer, but you don't particularly want them to have access to your files (or each other's). And this is what we'll look at next.

17.2 Adding a user

Let's imagine your daughter needs to use the Mac for her college coursework.

1 Make sure the padlock, bottom left, is unlocked so that you can make changes.

Click the lock to prevent further changes.

2 Click the **New Account** ('+') button bottom left.

3 This opens the New Account panel with a series of boxes that must be filled in. First, though, note the pop-up menu at the top. This lists the account types available. The most powerful is an *Administrator* account, but since you want to be the only one able to control the Mac's settings, you should choose *Standard* instead.

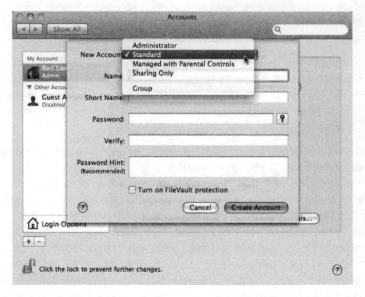

4 First, type in the new user's name. The **Short Name** box below will be filled in automatically.

5 Now type in a **Password** and confirm it in the box below and, just to be on the safe side, a **password hint** in the box at the bottom. Click on **Create Account** to finish.

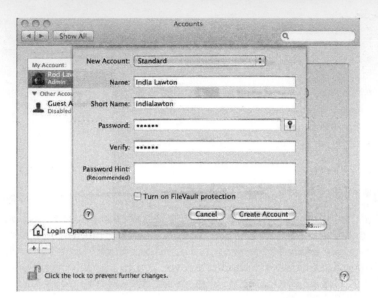

There are two significant aspects to what you've just done. The first is that when the Mac is started up, it will display both users on the screen, so that either of you can log on (it will require the correct password for each user account).

The second thing to note is that the new user has their own home folder with their own *Pictures* folder, *Music* folder, *Documents* folder and more. Each user can use the Mail application, for example, but they'll only ever see their own mail, and no one else's.

Other people's home folders are visible in the Finder in the *Users* folder, but only the current user's home folder has the home icon, and access to the others is barred.

Privacy is taken very seriously in the Mac OS. Even those with Administrator accounts can't access the contents of users' home folders without their password. Of course, you could always insist you choose the password when you create the account, but the more democratic thing to do is turn your back for a moment while the new user types it in.

There is a way for different users to exchange files, though, and that's via *Drop Boxes*. There is actually one folder in another user's home folder which you *can* access. First, open their *Public* folder. You'll see a *Drop Box* folder – you can drag items into this. Similarly, other users can leave items for you in your own Drop Box.

Different users can't see each other's files, but they can exchange files using the other person's Drop Box.

17.3 Switching between users

It's very useful for different people to be able to use the same computer while still keeping their files private, but it would be a nuisance if you had to shut down and restart the computer each time. Fortunately, you don't have to. You can switch users while the machine is running, and there are two ways of doing this:

1 Open the **Apple** menu and choose **Log Out**. This closes any applications currently running and returns you to the Login window and its list of users.

2 The quicker option is to go back to the System Preferences and the **Accounts** panel, unlock the padlock in the bottom left and click **Login Settings**. Now check the **Enable fast user switching** box.

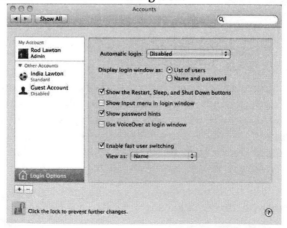

3 You'll see the current user's name at the right-hand end of the menu bar at the top of the screen. When you click this, you'll see a list of all the users. To switch users, click another name.

The Mac will prompt you for that user's password, then switch to 'their Mac'. With fast switching, each user's documents and applications remain open, so you can switch back to the previous user and they can pick up exactly where they left off.

Indeed, when you set up multiple user accounts, it really is as if each person has their own Mac. The whole process of setting up accounts and passwords may sound a bit of a nuisance, but it's simpler and quicker than it sounds and really is the perfect solution for a 'family' computer.

Summary

- You have a user account even if you are the only person who uses your Mac.

- It's best to disable automatic login, because if you don't anyone can start up your Mac.

- Only those with Administrator accounts can change important Mac settings.

- Individual users' files are kept private, which is ideal for family computers.

- Users can share their files through a Drop Box.

- With fast user switching it takes just moments for one user to take over from another.

8 System Preferences

In this chapter you will learn:

- how to configure and personalize your Mac's display

- about screen savers and customizing the Dock

- about hardware preferences

- how to activate the Mac's speech options

- how to apply parental controls to user accounts

- how to make a Mac easier to use for those with visual or hearing impairments

18.1   Personal Preferences

The Mac's System Preferences are mentioned many times throughout this book, and they're used to control many aspects of the Mac, like the Control Panel on a Windows PC. Many of these will never need changing, but it's still useful to know what they're for. They're split into four sections, and the first is devoted largely to the Mac's appearance and behaviour. You can configure these to customize your Mac.

Appearance

Many people will use their Macs for months or years without knowing (or caring, perhaps) that it's possible to change the look

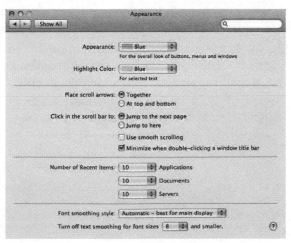

of parts of the interface. Here, though, you can change the colours used for highlighting, the position of scrollbars and the way text is rendered on the screen.

Desktop & Screen Saver

Here you can choose from a wide range of abstract desktop patterns or colours. (You can also set a desktop image directly from iPhoto.) If you don't like the standard screen saver (it can start to pall after a while), change it for another, like *Word of the Day*, which puts random definitions on the screen.

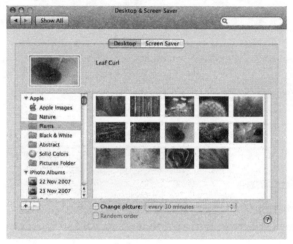

Dock

Normally, the Dock runs along the bottom of the screen, but you can align it vertically to the left- or right-hand sides. If you check the **Magnification** box, icons enlarge as you move the

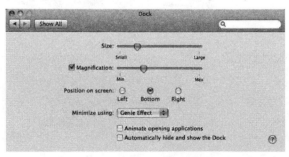

mouse pointer over them, which can be fun (for a while). And if you check the **Automatically hide and show the Dock** box, it slides out of the way when you're not using it and only reappears when you move the mouse pointer to the bottom of the screen.

Expose & Spaces

Expose is a Finder tool for showing all your open windows at once. It does this by shrinking them and displaying them side-by-side on the screen. This makes it easier to locate and switch to a window when there are lots open at once. Normally, you press [F9] to make this happen, but you can change this so that just moving the mouse pointer to the corners of the screen will do it. Also, this is where you configure the Spaces feature.

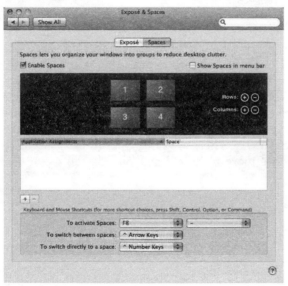

International

The language for your Mac will be set up when you first configure it, but it's also possible to change the language settings here later on.

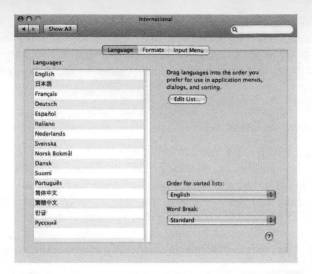

Security

There are three tabs in the Security panel. In the **General** tab (amongst other things) you can set the Mac to request a user password whenever it's woken from sleep or screensaver mode. And in the **FileVault** tab you can opt to encrypt your home folder so that the data cannot be viewed without a password – the encryption is stronger than regular user passwords and applied in a different way. There are other options in the Security panel, but they are more technical and outside the scope of a basic guide.

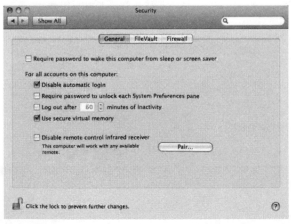

Spotlight

This is the Finder's search tool, and it will look in the listed locations for the words you type. You can deselect the areas you don't want to search, to save time or because they are irrelevant.

18.2 Hardware Preferences

Bluetooth

This is used to check the configuration of any Bluetooth devices connected to the Mac. The most obvious example of this is the wireless version of Apple's Mighty Mouse.

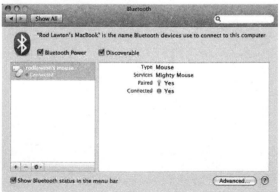

CDs & DVDs

In this panel you decide what you want the Mac to do when you insert a blank CD or DVD. By default, for example, the Mac opens blank CDs in the Finder but asks you what you want to do with blank DVDs. If you want these to open in the Finder too, or in another application, you choose that option from the pop-up menu alongside.

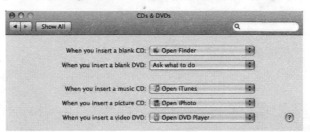

Displays

LCD displays only have one native resolution, and this will be selected automatically by the Mac. However, there may be instances where you need to select a lower resolution for screenshots to illustrate an article, for example. In the *Color* tab it's possible to manually calibrate the brightness and colour of your display against on-screen samples. This can help you get more accurate colours from some displays.

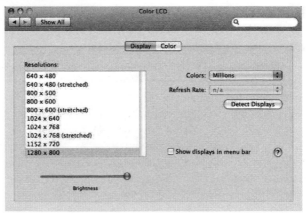

Energy Saver

Macs have different Energy Saver settings according to the model type and the situation. These are probably most useful with MacBooks and MacBook Pros, where you need to preserve battery power carefully when away from a mains supply. Using this panel you can set the Mac to go to sleep, set the display to sleep or power down the hard drive if it's not been used for a few minutes (the delay can be adjusted over a wide range).

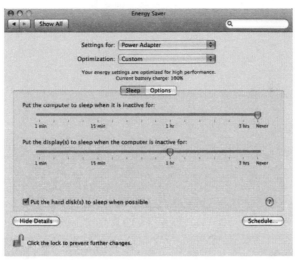

Keyboard & Mouse

You may never need to change any of these settings, but at least you'll know where they are and what they do. If you struggle with the Trackpad on a MacBook, use the **Trackpad** tab to experiment with the tracking speed and other settings. You can use the **Mouse** tab to reconfigure the mouse buttons and change the double-click speed. And if your Mac loses contact with your wireless Mighty Mouse (this happens if you switch the mouse off or move it out of range), you can re-establish contact with the **Bluetooth** panel.

Print & Fax

This panel shows any printers connected to the Mac and, if there's more than one, you can choose the *default*. This is the printer that appears first when you attempt to print from any application. If you click the **Options & Supplies** button, it may also be possible to check how much ink is remaining.

Sound

In the Sound panel's **Sound Effects** tab you can try out different alert sounds for your Mac, and in the **Output** tab it's possible to change the left–right balance of the speakers and the output volume – though you can also check the **Show volume in menu bar**

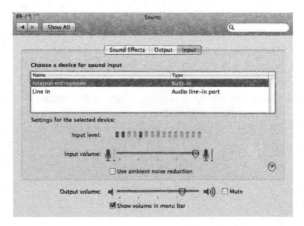

option so that the volume control is available all the time (besides, Mac keyboards have volume control keys anyway). The **Input** tab allows you to adjust the input volume of the built-in microphone and that of the Mac's *Line in* input, where used.

18.3   Internet & Network Preferences

These Preferences control the Mac's network and Internet connections and how files and folders are shared with others.

.Mac

If you don't have a .Mac account, this panel is irrelevant. If you do, you can use it to check your account status, choose which items are *Synced* with .Mac and when, and monitor how much of your available iDisk space remains unused.

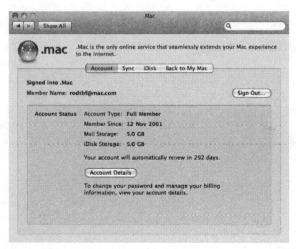

Network

The settings available here are technical and quite advanced, and with any luck you won't need to change any of them. The Mac connects to other networks automatically, but where you encounter problems and need to contact a technical support department, you may be asked to check and modify some of these settings.

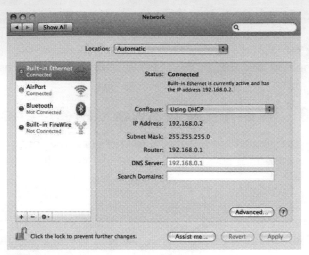

QuickTime

QuickTime is Apple's video playback program, and for the most part you can leave the default settings alone – it just works.

Sharing

This controls how some of the more advanced sharing tools are configured, e.g. whether other (authorized) users are allowed to view and control your computer remotely. Many users will want minimal sharing options, if any, and these can be selected from the list on the left. File Sharing, Printer Sharing and Bluetooth Sharing is probably as far as most people will want to go.

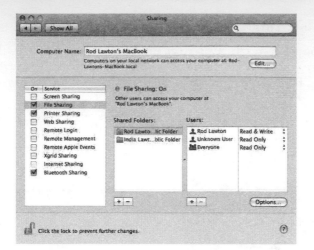

18.4 System Preferences

Here you can set up user accounts, set the Mac's internal date and time and adjust the operation of Leopard's Time Machine backup tool.

Accounts

We covered user accounts in some depth in Chapter 17, so we won't repeat it here. This is the panel where user accounts are set up and administered.

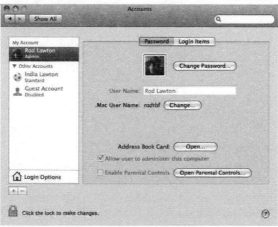

Date & Time

If you need to check or reset the Mac's date and time, this is where you do it. You can also configure the clock display on the menu bar, swapping from analogue to digital, for example.

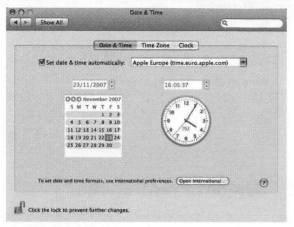

Parental Controls

If your Mac is used by many different family members, you may at one time or another be concerned about the websites they

might be visiting or how long they're spending on the computer. With this panel, you can modify each user account to carefully control this usage, and it's surprisingly easy to do.

Software Update

These days, applications don't wait for you to check whether updates are available. They check for you at regular intervals and prompt you to install any new updates. This applies to the Mac operating system too. Here you can configure how often update checks are made, and you can also examine a history of previously-installed updates (although for Apple software only).

Speech

It's possible to control your Mac and some of its applications using voice commands! It's not enabled as standard, though, because while this kind of technology is certainly a novelty, it

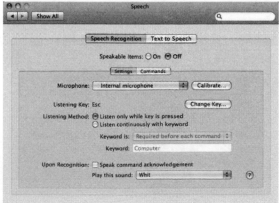

lacks the speed and precision of conventional mouse/keyboard input. Your Mac can also read out text in computer voices which make a good stab at sounding human, and there are several to choose from in the **Text to Speech** tab. Want to try it? Choose a key combination unlikely to be used by any other software (e.g. **[Ctrl]-[Alt]-[Command[-[S]]**). Select any text on the screen, use this key combination and wait for the Mac to start talking.

Startup Disk

You'll only need this panel if you're using Boot Camp to turn your Mac into a PC, or if you need to start up from a DVD or network drive to carry out diagnostics and fault-finding.

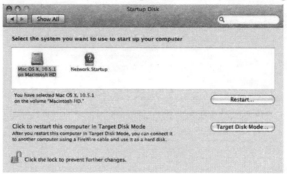

Time Machine

Time Machine is Leopard's brand new backup tool (see Section 4.8), and here you can switch it on or off and choose the external disk drive used for the backups.

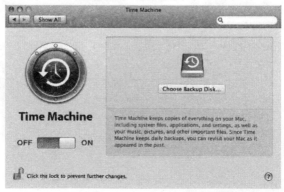

Universal Access

The Mac has a number of options for helping those with eyesight or hearing difficulties. It can display text larger on the screen, read out options when the mouse pointer is moved over them and flash the screen instead of playing an alert sound.

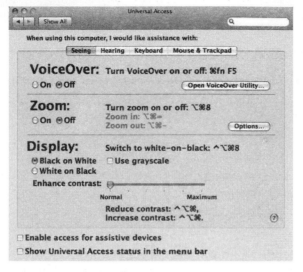

Summary

+ The System Preferences consist of a series of panels for configuring different aspects of the Mac.

+ System Preferences are split into four main areas which control the Mac's appearance, hardware devices, Internet and network connections and miscellaneous System settings.

+ Many System Preferences can be left at their defaults unless problems occur.

glossary

Airport   Apple's name for the Mac's wireless networking hardware. It hooks up seamlessly to standard PC wireless networks and routers.

Bit   The basic building block of digital data. A bit is either 1 or 0, but by stringing bits together it's possible to store much more complex data.

Blog   A web journal where new entries are posted regularly and old entries are stored in a searchable archive.

Bluetooth   A short-range wireless communications system that's not fast enough for proper networks or Internet connection, but fine for things like wireless keyboards and mice.

Broadband   Modern digital communications system using conventional phone lines but with digital data transfer that's much faster than old-fashioned modems.

Burn   CDs store data optically not magnetically, so you can't save data to them in the same way you'd save it to a floppy disk. The data has to be burned (literally) into the surface

Byte   8 *bits* strung together. One bit has only two possible values, one byte has 256.

Clock speed   The number of processing cycles a processor carries out each second. It's a good indicator of a processor's performance when compared with another of the same type.

Combo drive   A CD-ROM drive that can also read DVDs and burn CDs. If you want to burn DVDs too, you need a Mac with a *superdrive*.

Context menu or shortcut menu, one devoted to specific objects on the screen and activated by clicking the right mouse button or holding down [Ctrl] when you click the left button.

Dialog A window which prompts you for more information or to make a choice. For example, when you save a file, the Save dialog will ask you what you want to call it and where you want to save it.

Dial-up conection Pre-broadband Internet connection where the computer's *modem* would have to dial up the Internet host computer over the telephone line.

Driver A software tool which allows hardware devices to communicate with the computer. Many devices come with software, including drivers, which you must install before they can be used.

Ethernet Networking system for computers in the same room or building. May be wireless or wired (using cables).

File sharing Making files on one computer accessible to other computers on the network.

Firewire A means of connecting computers and peripherals. Similar to USB, but the two are incompatible. Now rarely used, though still a standard way of transferring footage from digital camcorders.

Folder A container for files and other folders on a computer and a way of keeping things organized. Rather like the folders in a filing cabinet, but here you can have folders within folders within folders and so on.

Freeware Software which is given away, usually by programmers trying to make a name for themselves or as a promotional tool for software companies.

FTP (File Transfer Protocol) A standard system for managing files and folders on a host computer over the Internet.

Gigahertz A measurement of *clock speed* in a computer. Today, 1 gigahertz (GHz) is on the slow side, 2Ghz is good, but faster is better.

Hardware The physical bits of the computer – circuit boards, screens, keyboards, printers.

iLink   Another name for Firewire, a standard way of connecting camcorders to computers.

Ken Burns effect   Adds the appearance of motion to still images by slow panning and zooming and subtle transitions.

Menu bar   A list of menu titles running horizontally across the top of the screen. You click on a menu title to display the menu.

Minimize The yellow button in the top left-hand corner of a window shrinks it into a little icon on the Dock. The window hasn't gone away – you can click the icon to show it again.

Modem   Device which converts computer data into a form which can be transmitted across telephone lines, and back again into data. May be built into the computer or plugged in as an external device.

Navigate   Move from one location (folder) on your hard disk to another, either within a program in an application, or within the Finder.

Operating system   If the computer's hardware is its body, this is its brain. You, and the programs you use, interact with the operating system, which then controls the hardware. From time to time, manufacturers will upgrade this operating system with new tools for fixes for things that didn't work properly.

Palette   A collection of tools or an informational display which can be moved around the screen into the most convenient position or closed completely when it's not needed.

Peripheral   Any external device you plug into a computer.

Podcast   Audio or video programme which is made available for downloading from the Internet rather than broadcast. So called because it was originally conceived by Apple as broadcasts for the iPod.

POP email accounts   POP is the standard protocol for handling email messages which you download to your computer using an email program.

RAM (Random Access Memory)   The computer's temporary thinking space. Most computers are shipped with the bare minimum, and adding more can speed up many processes.

Router A device which handles the data traffic between computers on a network, routing it to the right machines.

Scrollbar These appear at the right and the base of a window when it's too small to show the full contents of the file. You can use the scrollbars to see the other parts of the file.

Search engine A website whose sole purpose is to help you find information on other websites. You type in a word or phrase and the search engine finds all the sites that mention it.

Shareware Software that's distributed freely, but which you're expected to pay for if you want to carry on using it once you've tried it out.

Sidebar Vertical panel on the left of the screen in many Mac programs, which is designed to offer quick access to common tools or locations.

Sleep mode Reduced-power mode where the computer powers down the display and drive, but doesn't actually shut down. When you 'wake' it, you can start work just where you left off.

Spam Unsolicited email which is trying to sell you things, tempt you with get-rich-quick schemes or, occasionally, trying to trick you into giving personal details ('phishing').

Stick drive Solid state memory devices which plug directly into a USB port and can be used for transferring files to other computers. Usually no larger than a small key fob.

Superdrive A drive which can read and write both CDs and DVDs. Found on most new Macs but not all (cheaper models may have *combo drives* which can't write DVDs).

Surfing Browsing the Web, generally with no particular destination in mind.

Terabyte We're used to measuring hard disk capacity in gigabytes (millions of megabytes), but some drives are now over 1,000 gigabytes – and 1000Gb is a terabyte.

Toolbar Horizontal strip of buttons and drop-down menus, usually displayed below the menu bar and designed for a specific and related set of operations. You might have a toolbar for adjusting text formatting in a word processor, for example.

USB interface A standard means of connecting computers to external devices. A USB cable connects the USB socket on the device to the USB port on the computer.

Virtual memory If the computer doesn't have enough random access memory to complete a task, it temporarily transfers some data to the hard disk to make room. This is virtual memory – it's not quite the same as the real thing, being dramatically slower, for a start.

Widget Small software tool designed to do a simple job quickly.

Wireless hotspot Any area within wireless range of a router or other access point with an Internet connection.

index